HOW TO DRAW UP YOUR OWN PEACEFUL SETTLEMENT AGREEMENT WITH YOUR SPOUSE.

The National Marital Settlement Kit

By Benji O. Anosike, B.B.A., M.A., Ph.D.

Library of Congress Cataloging-in-Publication Data

Anosike, Benji O.
How to draw up your own peaceful settlement agreement with your spouse : the national marital settlement kit / by Benji O. Anosike.
p. cm.
Includes bibliographical references and index.
ISBN 0-932704-55-7 (alk.paper)
1. Divorce settlements--United States--Popular works. 2. Separation (Law)--United States--Popular works. I. Title.

KF535.Z9 A563 2001
346.7301'66--dc21 2001028754

Printed in the United States of America
ISBN: 0-932704-55-7
Library of Congress Catalog Number:

Published by:
Do-It-Yourself Legal Publishers
60 Park Place
Newark, NJ 07102

Table of Contents

Chapter 7
LET'S SIGN THE WRITTEN AGREEMENT: THE PROCEDURES FOR THE ALL-IMPORTANT "EXECUTION" OF THE AGREEMENT

Chapter 8
EVERY QUESTION YOU MAY WANT TO HAVE ANSWERED ON HETEROSEXUAL/HOMOSEXUAL COHABITATION, THE "MARVIN CASE", AND PROPERTY RIGHTS OF NON-MARITAL COUPLES

Chapter 9
TAX CONSIDERATIONS IN SEPARATION & SETTLEMENT AGREEMENTS

APPENDICES

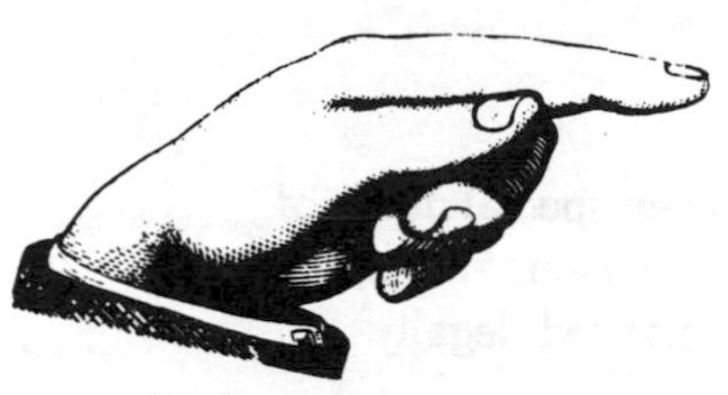

FOREWORD:
THE PUBLISHER'S MESSAGE

To All Our Dear Readers:

This manual is consciously conceived and written with one fundamental objective in mind: for "preventive" law purposes, to spare you the necessity of ever having to go through the all-too-familiar expenses and emotional drains of what could be a lengthy and bitter court battle for a divorce[1], separation, or property settlement,somewhere down the road.

Using this manual, you can readily draft an appropriate contract with your partner, without a lawyer's involvement; and save yourself the lawyer's hefty legal fees while getting essentially the same quality product — upwards of $500 for the simplest type of agreement, and repeated charges each time there's a revision or an amendment to be made! BUT THERE'S A MUCH MORE INVALUABLE "SAVINGS" YOU MAKE FROM USING THIS BOOK: the incalculable financial and emotional problems you could save yourself only because a timely contract with that lady or gentleman of your momentary romantic fancy later works to keep you out of the courtrooms and lawyers' offices.

Why seek a Written Couples' Agreement?

As one New York lawyer and author experienced in matrimonial cases aptly put it, "a contract with your loved ones could [later] keep you out of court and/or the poorhouse!"

And yet another thoughtful lawyer, Toni Kara, a California matrimonial specialist and author on the subject, put it this way, explaining why it's easier but most advisable that couples have a written agreement: "Fortunately, [unlike the situation with commercial type contracts and lease documents], living-together agreements are different. You are free to design your agreement to say exactly what you want, in words that you can understand... And writing down your expectations is... the best way to stay out of court. Given our adversary domestic relation system, any money or property that exists at the start of a court fight almost always gets consumed by the lawyers. [Hence], in the end, personal disputes [potential or actual], can only be solved well by the people involved."[2]

The central point, in a word, is that you do yourself a great favor and save yourself (and your spouse and probably children) a world of time, trouble, and your hard-earned money, by simply endeavoring to resolve, relatively peacefully and privately, any issues or disputed matters between you and your spouse — rather than, in effect, guaranteeing that they'll wind up in the lawyer's offices and the court rooms at assured multiples the time, hassles and costs, to you!

This manual tells you, quite simply, that there is one primary legal safeguard and preventive measure available today which you had better used: A GOOD WRITTEN AGREEMENT with your spouse or mate!

With this present manual as a guide, you shall have escaped the fate of millions who are destined to fall into the developing social dragnet of the modern times in America, when interpersonal relationship fail or falter. You shall have been able to work out an amicable and agreeable settlement of terms with your spouse or mate to make for a more civilized and far less acrimonious and expensive divorce or separation.

---

[1] **The companion volumes by this Publisher, *"How to Do Your Own Divorce Without a Lawyer,"* a multi-volume series, provides interested readers with the same facility with regard to procedures for actually filing for a divorce yourself. The national edition of this manual is packaged for use in almost every state.**

[2] Quoted from "The People's Law Review" ed. Ralph Warner (1980) pp. 97-8

The guidebook, carefully written and tailored to be all-inclusive, fits the different, even special needs of almost everyone involved in male-female or relationships of any kind, whether they be persons who are happily married, or about to embark on a divorce or dissolution action; or are engaged-to-be-married, legally separated.[3]

Never Mind, You Can and May Draw up the Papers Yourself - Just as Safely, Competently.

At this stage in the nation's legal history, most people probably know this by now: namely, that it is a basic civil and constitutional *right* of every American, who so chooses, to act as his or her own "attorney" in any civil matters (which obviously includes the drawing up of matrimonial or living-together papers and agreements). Sure, lawyers have traditionally been looked to to draw up matrimonial agreements, and they can still be useful in a limited way, in some of those undertakings. But in this era of a growing public attitude of let's-cut-down-on-the-rising-costs-by-doing-some-of-it-ourselves, what's more to the point today is this simple fact: *not only is there no law which says that to be legal a marital or cohabitation agreement must be drawn up by a person titled a "lawyer," but there is also no commonsense reason why it could be so.* The truth is that any marital or cohabitation agreement (or, for that matter, any agreement of any kind whatsoever) which meets the simply common sense requirements of clarity, fairness, inclusiveness and evenhandedness, is just as legally valid as any other agreement — whether or not it be drawn up by you, the "lay person," or by the best lawyer that Harvard has ever turned out, or even by your house dog!

To sum it all up in one sentence, what it all boils down to, then, is this: do you have enough knowledge of the basic law, and of what constitutes the essential elements of a valid agreement to be able to draw up, by yourself, a document that meets your own basic needs? THIS IS THE BASIC MATTER THAT THIS MANUAL, WHILE DEMYSTIFYING THE LAW, IS OUT TO HELP YOU WITH.

The Changing "New Morality" of These Times Demand Precautionary Legal Measure!

Yet, in this Publisher's humble assessment, never has such an instructional guidebook on the subject been more necessary or timely. With the current trend in America's social and matrimonial scene today, with the escalating trend towards instability and unpredictability in relationships, sooner or later every American involved in a living-together situation of any sort would probably need some form of written agreement with the partner. Time was—indeed, it was a few short decades ago—when it would have been unthinkable, for example, to even conceive of matters like money, property division, let alone inheritance or divorce, as issues for discussion between lovers engaged to be married. Marriage was, in those "good old days," strictly a social and moral issue, completely divorced from business and monetary considerations.

Not so any more, though! Today, as Max Lichtenberg, a New York matrimonial lawyer, put it, *"Marriage is no longer viewed as something made in heaven by angels. It's (now viewed as) a legal contract with emotions terminating." And since there has been a marked lessening in the emotional contents of marital relationships, the focus of the emphasis has therefore shifted to exactly those very items which would have been criminal to even think about in years gone by: MONEY, who gets to keep what property if you should ever break up or die, and things of this sort.*[4]

---

[3] See footnote on page 69 for relevant statistics on the dramatic upward trend in the number of cohabitating couples, divorce rates, and rates of non-remarriage after divorce. A report in the *New York Times* (January 1979) reported, for example, that since the nation's premier cohabitation case, California's famous "Marvin case," was decided in 1976, "hundreds of former lovers in New York and 15 other states have filed similar suits alleging that they are entitled to everything from alimony to pension rights."

[4] Drs. Philip Blumstein and Pepper Schwartz, sociologists at the University of Washington who conducted a National Science Foundation-backed research on the secrets of compatibility among couples, found there's a trend toward expressing verbalized arrangements among married couples and unmarried persons just living together alike, involving specifically negotiated allocations of money and more economic independence reserved by the individuals. "There's less of 'what's mine is yours and what's yours is mine,' " they reported.

"Because couples are focusing less on emotional issues today, the accountant and the appraisal of property are much more important than they used to be," said Ruth Miller, Chairman of the California Bar Association, recently.

The Causes of the "New Morality" and What Lessons From it

And what brought about this trend towards unpredictability in relationships? Experts have attempted to explain it in terms of any number of factors: prevalence of liberalized "no-fault" divorce laws and philosophies across the nation, women's liberation, increased mobility of Americans, financial affluence and increased leisure time, changed social mores concerning loyalty and stability in marital, employment, and social relationships, generally; decrease in the moral influence of the church; the media and advertising promotion of the grass-is-always-greener-elsewhere idea; the coming of age of the post-Vietnam "me generation" of young couples, and so on and so forth. Whatever the real reasons, however, what is far more clear have been the **results and the underlying implication** of the new trend: Those relationships which used to be permanent ties, or at least lasting ties, are now easily severed; people are now more frequently inclined to (and frequently do) engage in informal coupling, casual partnership changing, and an attitude of little concern toward entering and getting out of relationships of all types, and given these modern realities, you'd be a dammed fool not to safeguard and protect yourself**!.**

The Central Message: Safeguard and Protect Yourself

The central message is rather clear, then: The current climate is one that makes it increasingly important, even necessary, to reduce relationships and understandings to writing. And anyone who ignores that reality does so at his or her own risk!! (It is no accident, for example, that more and more divorce judgments and terms of court settlements are increasingly being based on written "stipulations" and agreements previously worked out by the parties.) This book gives you all the tools and knowledge you need to be able to do just that, yourself—competently, and without too much expense or redtape. It's "preventive" law at its best!

Nor do you necessarily have to actually have a formal agreement, or to "do it yourself," for this book to be useful to or necessary for you. Not at all! In the end, even if you were to decide to hire a lawyer to do it for you, yet by doing your homework on it and doing some of the preliminary work yourself, you would have been able to save yourself substantial amount of money. Even more importantly, you shall have become far better educated and informed about your options, even if you choose never to take advantage of them, and, at the very least, just being educated on the subject matter provides you with the opportunity to make an informed choice.

The Publisher's Continuing Gratitude To You, The Reader

Finally, we urge this of you, our readers: Please send us any comments, opinions or suggestions you might have regarding this manual. Just drop us a few lines at our publishing offices. (We prefer written communication, please.) With us, YOU, our readers, are the KING and QUEEN! We value and welcome your feedback --always!!

Thank You

The Publishers,
—Do-it-Yourself Legal Publishers,

CHAPTER 1

SOME IMPORTANT BACKGROUND CONCEPTS IN LIVING-TOGETHER RELATIONSHIPS AND CONTRACTS

The following terms are defined[1] below, just for the purpose of setting the stage for the materials in the later chapters:

1) Legal Marriage
2) Common-Law Marriage
3) Putative Marriage
4) Legal Separation
5) Settlement Agreement
6. Ante-Nuptial Agreement
7) Cohabitation
8) Homosexual live-Along
9) Palimony

1. Legal Marriage

Every reader of this manual probably has a pretty good idea of what a marriage is all about. But let's just define it here, however, for the purposes of this manual. Briefly, we define marriage here as the status of a man and a woman who have been legally united as a husband and wife for the prime purpose of establishing a family; the union of two persons of opposite sex by civil contract, in which they assume a status granted by the State.

The most important things to bear in mind in a (legal) definition of marriage are basically two-fold: first, that it is a "contract;" and second, that unlike most other contracts, it is one of the few contracts in which parties other than the contracting parties themselves, in this case the State, have a stake. In every legal marriage, the state is said to be a "silent partner" to the marriage contract. It is by the laws of the state (and by that only) that the final results of the rights and obligations of the parties to a marriage contract are fixed, changed or dissolved. Hence, each state has its own requirements for contracting a legal marriage (licenses, medical exams, age of consent, etc.), as well as the requirements by which the relationship may be dissolved or the marital property distributed or inherited.

2. Common-Law Marriage

This is a relationship or arrangement, a much less informal one than a legally contracted marriage, whereby a man and a woman live together and conduct themselves as man and wife *without* formalizing or solemnizing the relationship. Certain states recognize this relationship as a valid marriage while others do not.

States which permit common-law marriages include: Alabama, Colorado, District of Columbia, Georgia, Idaho, Iowa, Kansas, Montana, Ohio, Oklahoma, Pennsylvania, Rhode Island, South Carolina and Texas. The criteria for common-law marriages vary from state to state.

[1] For definition of terms, general, see the Glossary of Legal Terms, Appendix B.

Generally, it is sufficient if the man and woman live and share their lives together and generally "hold themselves out to the public" as husband and wife. The most common criteria are using the same last name, referring to each other as husband and wife, filing joint income tax returns, opening joint bank accounts, and listing both names on the birth certificate of their children, etc.

3. Putative Marriage

This is a relationship wherein a man and a woman live together, with either one of them or both believing in honest good faith, that they are lawfully married, while, in fact, they really aren't. Example: A woman enters into a marital relationship with a man who claims to have been divorced from his previous wife, while the fact is that he actually wasn't divorced; or, he enters into such a relationship in the honest belief that the man she had previously been married to was dead, when in fact he was not.

4. Legal Separation

The state of living apart by a husband and wife either by a valid written agreement or by a decree (and order) of separation issued by a court. (More on this topic in Chapters 2, 4 & 5)

5. Settlement Agreement

An agreement (same as a "contract"), sometimes by spoken words but usually in writing, between two persons in a married, quasi-married, or cohabitation relationship, by which the parties set out the property rights and entitlements of each other in the event of death or termination of the relationship. (More on this topic in Chapter 4.)

6. Pre-Nuptial Agreement

Conventionally, this is an agreement (same as a "contract") made between a man and a woman at any time before they subsequently married, usually centering around issues of the rights and entitlements each would have with respect to their property. Same thing as "ante-nuptial" or "pre-marriage" agreement or contract. (More on this topic in Appendix D.)

7. Cohabitation

This is the current term generally used to describe the relatively novel but growing phenomenon of two persons of opposite sex living together as partners, roommates, friends, or lovers without being married to each other. (More on this topic in Chapter 8.)

8. Homosexual (Gay and Lesbian) Live-Alongs

This is generally conceived of as the act of living together by two (or more) persons of the SAME sex, not merely as roommates or business partners, but as sexual partners and lovers. When persons involved are female, it's called a "lesbian" relationship, and when they are male it's a "gay" relationship. The relevant rules or living-together agreement which this type of relationships would come under would be the "cohabitation" procedures. (See Chapter 8.)

9. Palimony

This is essentially a term for alimony paid to a live-in lover or "pal" after a relationship had ended. Arising out of the now-famous 1976 Marvin case of California, the logic behind the concept was simple: Since the unmarried partner often fills substantially the same role as a spouse — ranging from taking care of the house, to bearing or raising children and ministering to and providing companionship to a partner— isn't it only fair and logical that he or she should, upon the termination of the relationship, be entitled to a share of the property accumulated during the live-in relationship, just as a married partner would upon a divorce? The Marvin case established, though, that in California (as in most states), there's no such thing as palimony for non-married people in the sense of a statutory duty of support; that, instead, if there is to be any support, it has to arise out of an actual contractual agreement made between two people. Thus, came about the legal significance of entering into a written settlement or cohabitation agreement between partners, whether married or unmarred! (See Chapter 8 for more on this.)

CHAPTER 2

DOING YOUR COHABITATION, SEPARATION OR SETTLEMENT AGREEMENT: WHY (AND WHEN) YOU SHOULD DO IT YOURSELF WITHOUT A LAWYER

A. Why You Not Only Can, But Should Write Your Own Agreement, Without A Lawyer

The preliminary question for us here in this chapter is not whether you can, as a non-lawyer, draw up a valid or competent cohabitation or marital settlement agreement. That question has been addressed and adequately laid to rest elsewhere (see page 35). Rather, the question here is even more basic: the practical and strategic reason why it is necessary, indeed advantageous, for you that you negotiate and drawn up the agreement yourselves, rather than involving an attorney.

B. Settlement Agreements are Primarily a Tool for Attaining Less-than-hostile Divorce Breakup

As is amply illustrated elsewhere in this guidebook (see pp. 31-33), ultimately the fundamental reason for which cohabitation and marriage-related property or settlement agreements of sorts are drafted or employed in the modern family law practice, is practical — essentially to make an eventual breakup, if and when one were to come, less costly or hurtful, financially, emotionally and otherwise. Its prime object, in a word, is as a tool for "planning" or "negotiating" an eventual divorce (or a breakup, in the case of unmarried parties who are merely cohabiting), if that should become necessary.

C. Can You Be Your Own "Attorney" Even In Divorce?

The subject of divorce proper is, of course, beyond the scope of the present manual; it is treated elsewhere.* However, in this chapter we shall merely address the general conditions you'd need to have if you are to ensure that you will be in the best possible position to successfully and easily process your own divorce case — that is, primarily by making sure to have a good marital settlement agreement.

There's a simple test to the question: 'Can you do your own divorce?' Let's put it this way: If you can simply read and understand just this manual, and are able generally to make simple practical decisions, follow clear and easy instructions, and fill out simple, standard forms, then you can quite easily do your own divorce (or dissolution of marriage). **IT'S THAT SIMPLE!**

---

*Readers who are interested in the subject of divorce may consult the nation-wide 10-volume series on the subject, "How to Do Your Own Divorce Without a Lawyer," written by the same author and published by the Selfhelper Law Press of America, a subsidiary of Do-It-Yourself Legal Publishers.

On the other hand, as a practical matter, there are just a few situations where it simply may not be advisable for you to do your own divorce or dissolution. These would be in a situation where:

(a) your spouse actually hires an attorney in a divorce case, and then actually files legal papers to oppose you; and/or where

(b) your spouse is presently on active military duty **and** will not cooperate with you and sign a WAIVER form granting that he'll not contest the divorce.

In brief, if your case does NOT come under one of the two exceptions listed above (if there's no lawyer involved in the case and no active military status by the other spouse), and you are honestly certain, after you've read this book, that you have no trouble following simple instructions or making simple practical decisions or compromises, then you can almost certainly do your own divorce — with all ease and facility.

D. What to Look For In Deciding Whether To Be Your Own "Attorney"

First of all, get it perfectly clear: with respect to divorce or other civil matters (e.g., settlement agreements and the like), the law says that it is your right to have an attorney represent you, if and when that is what you prefer and want to do, or NOT to have one represent you, if you don't prefer or want to. AND NO LAW WHATSOEVER EVER SAYS THAT YOU MUST HAVE A LAWYER REPRESENT YOU. That's the Law! It's pretty simple to decide whether or not you need an attorney. The rule-of-thumb is simple: basically, in divorce (or other civil) cases, if your spouse is not putting up a legal "contest" (legal fight or opposition) against the proposed settlement or divorce suit, whichever is applicable, you probably don't need an attorney. And, in fact, as you will soon learn below, there are big advantages to not having or involving a lawyer in a case, in any event.

Thus, in a matter involving a cohabitation or marital property settlement, so long as the matter is an amicable one between the parties, then you and your partner can just as easily act as your own attorneys and draw up your own agreements with no lawyer involvement. Now, what if it were a divorce that is involved? In such a situation, to be your own attorney in the case, it's most ideal and desirable if and when there is NO opposition (legal opposition) at all from your spouse, if and when the case is "uncontested". *Perhaps your spouse is long gone from the house, or for some reason he has no particular interest in what you may do. Or, he or she, too, wants the divorce as badly as you do.* In such a case, you will probably have a very easy time doing your own divorce or dissolution. Where, on the other hand, your spouse is in the family picture and cares about what happens, you should make an effort to talk things over with him and try to agree on basic things. This is because there are important advantages for you in working things out. Also, being suddenly served with legal papers without prior warning or information might send your spouse the unintended signal and send him running to a lawyer, and thereby get the two of you involved in unnecessary legal tangles and expenditures none of you really wanted but which you'd be unable to stop once it's set in motion!

BUT WHAT IF, ON THE OTHER HAND, YOU HAVE TRIED YOUR HARDEST and you can't work things out, but you are nevertheless not certain whether or not your spouse will actually put up any legal opposition against a divorce action (maybe all that noise is just a bluff)? In such a situation, a wise strategy may be for you to still go ahead and start the divorce case on your own anyway. See what happens. If your spouse does then actually get an attorney who then proceeds to file legal papers in court to oppose your action, then you will have to get an attorney, too — at that point, but only *then.*

As a practical matter, a situation when you definitely ought not attempt to do your own divorce, is when a spouse is on active military duty but would not cooperate with you by signing the consent or waiver paper for you. In such a situation, either wait for him to get out of the military, or get an attorney. However, if your military spouse will cooperate with you just to the extent of signing a consent paper (something called a "Waiver") to let the divorce proceed, then it's alright and you can still proceed as your own divorce attorney just as well.

E. There Are Definite Advantages To Being Your Own Attorney

First Advantage: It's Much Cheaper Doing It Yourself

Perhaps the most obvious advantage of doing your own written agreement or your own dissolution (divorce), is the dramatic SAVINGS IN COST. On divorce, for example, a New York City Department of Consumer Affairs survey in 1992 reported that the lawyers' fees for doing just a simple uncontested dissolution ranged from $600 to $1500, with most falling between $400 and $700, not including the out-of pocket costs and charges, such as the filing fee, cost of serving the papers, and the like, which separately averaged over $300. Many attorneys argue that they have to charge that much because, they claim, few cases stay uncontested! In deed, they have a point; in almost every case where one spouse gets an attorney involved, the other spouse will almost surely run out and get one too, and the legal cost will then be at least DOUBLE!

Here's how Nancy E. Albert[1] , herself a practicing Chicago divorce Lawyer and author, summed up the prevailing fee practice and habit of her fellow lawyers:

> "Lawyers' fees vary dramatically. Few of the "downtown" lawyers will touch your case before you put $1,000 on the table. Many insist on a $2,000 "retainer" (advance fee). One Chicago firm advertises that they will do divorces for $50 plus costs, but when asked in person will respond that they charge $350 for their high volume, simple, uncontested divorces. A few lawyers advertise divorces for anywhere from $30 to $250, but may tell you that, while the advertised fee is for a simple divorce, your divorce is much more complicated, and will cost more. A standard fee for a simple, uncontested divorce charged by many lawyers is $750, plus court costs."

Yet, even at their often prohibitive prices, lawyers would generally not give you much time, attention or information, and this is especially true in the supposedly cut-rate law offices. You may find it very difficult to get personal advice and attention. You almost always end up wondering what's going on in a situation, but there's no one to talk to about it. **The point here, simply is this:** that as a general proposition, you can save at least $400, more like $600, and as much as $1200 or more, by doing it yourself!

SECOND ADVANTAGE: Without A Lawyer's Involvement You Can Better Keep It Simple

Most separating or divorcing couples start off with a simple case alright. But then, all of a sudden the case doesn't end up that way. Lawyers, many experts agree, have a way of making almost anything more complicated. This is primarily because of the way they are trained, the way they think, and the way the legal system works. A lawyer is, in a word, a combatant. Our system of justice is known as "the adversary system". The principles and attitudes we see in the courtrooms of today are said to have begun on the medieval field of honor where trial by combat meant that whoever survived in the end was "right."

Law schools generally have no course requirement in counseling or communication skills, and generally offer none. Instead, the training strongly emphasizes aggressive and defensive strategy and how to squeeze out the most financial advantage in every case. Is this the attitude you want in your divorce?

A New Mexico publication on the subject summed it up this way[2]:

> "Most dissolutions are fairly sensitive and it doesn't take much to stir things up. Your average attorney is just too likely to make things worse, instead of better. Here's a typical example. Let's say a couple is separated and they have things more or less stabilized, in a situation where lots of sleeping dogs are being left to lie. Then one spouse goes to an attorney to start the dissolution. Often the attorney encourages the client to ask for more property and support than is actually expected. Lawyers think it pays to ask for extra so they can bargain their way back down. When the other spouse hears of this, it's a big shock, and that person will feel deceived. There's tension and trouble, not to mention

---

[1] As quoted in "Insider's Guide To Divorce In Illinois: The Practical Consumer Divorce Manual" by Nancy E. Albert (Nancy E. Albert, Publisher, Evansville, Ill. 1984) at p. 33,

[2] "Uncontested Divorce Kit, New Mexico, "p.3.

mistrust and hurt. In most cases, just receiving formal legal documents from an attorney will motivate the other spouse to go see their own attorney for an independent opinion. Then the fun really starts.

The two attorneys start off costing just double, ***but pretty soon they start writing letters and filing motion and doing standard attorney-type things, just like they were taught. Now we have a contested case,*** more fees and charges, and a couple of very upset spouses. Sure hope they don't have kids. The fees in contested cases run from a lot all the way up to everything." (Emphasis added by the writer)

One veteran divorce lawyer, Gail J. Koff[3], a partner in the New York branch office of Jacoby & Meyers Law firm, while extolling the essentiality of the lawyer's involvement in marital settlement, concedes that such kinds of trouble-creating lawyers are prevalent whose main role in marital disputes is to build confrontation and exacerbate tensions between spouses in order to build up legal fees. Attorney Koff, obviously an avid advocate of attorney involvement in the handling of all marital agreements and divorce, contends, however, that that breed of lawyers was a major factor only in the past when fault based divorce was the law. But not any more, she says. True, said Attorney Koff, in that "past" era, the kind of lawyers who controlled the system were the ones whose "specialty was getting in there and then 'sticking it' to the opponent, often using intimidation as a potent weapon. More often than not these attorneys simply exacerbated the problems, sometimes forcing a formidable wedge between the spouses. But just as often, they were enormously effective and got the job done for their clients."

But, says Koff, the rules have since changed: "once fault was no longer an issue and the emphasis shifted from sin to economics, this brand of attorney went the way of the dinosaurs."

Koff's perspective is certainly not lacking in imagination and inventiveness! In substance, though, her account is grounded more in fiction or hope than in reality. For, even at the same time, even as she claims that the old rules have "changed", she's enthusiastic about the use by attorneys in her own firm of tactics that were purely a throwback to the same old adversarial order lawyers are noted for. For one thing, she endorsed the tactics of a lawyer in her firm who pressed on for shared custody, anyway, as a "negotiating tool" even though the client had perfectly been willing to settle for less, and another lawyer's tactics of calling in the police and accusing a parent of sexually molesting his own daughter in order to use the law as a "sword or as a shield" in a custody fight![4]

So, again, the point here remains simple: ***If you do your settlement or divorce yourself, you (and your spouse) are much more likely to keep a case that started out simple that way -- SIMPLE!***

THIRD ADVANTAGE: You'd Get A Unique Sense Of Personal Satisfaction Doing It Yourself

Admittedly, it's a bit more work for you if you do it yourself. But this way, though, you stand to understand every step. You are completely in charge of your own case, your own decisions, and your own life.

The beneficial fallouts of this aspect of doing your own dissolution is subtle and is, hence, often under-estimated. But for you, it can become the most important advantage of them all. Doing it yourself helps to overcome the helpless feeling that often comes at this time. It will focus your mind on the practical things, get you moving in a positive and constructive way, and give you a sense of movement out of the past and into the future. It feels good to stand on your

[3] Koff, Love and The Law: A Legal Guide To Relationships in the '90's, pp. 165-166. Another report, a more recent one to add its voice to the perennial debate, makes much the same point almost in identical words: "the simple addition of two lawyers to the problems encountered by a couple considering divorce will merely intensify any conflict.

The reason for this is rooted in the way that most lawyers approach divorce. They want to "win" a divorce...(and in this), they set up an enormously costly game of legal chess with the spouses and any children of a marriage as pawns in the game.

The legal maneuvering generally begins with the lawyer preparing a list of demands...The client is urged to ask for everything: the house, the car, custody of the children, huge amounts of alimony and child support, the household possessions...Of course, the other spouse will be outraged when confronted with such a list of demands and will immediately seek out a mercenary lawyer to draw up a list of equally outrageous counter-demands. Thus, the battle lines will have been drawn. The attempt to amicably dissolve a marriage and get on with one's life will have escalated into an economic and psychological war which will cause enormous suffering and long-term misery for the participants."

The report added: "(But) there is an alternative to turning a divorce into a war waged by competing lawyers...The alternative is a no-fault divorce by agreement." (Daniel Sitarz, a Florida attorney, in "Divorce Yourself" (Nova Publishing Co: 1991) pp. 11-12)

[4] Ibid. pp. 55-71. It should only be added that Koff concedes that individuals "may feel capable of writing their own separation agreement," but maintains that "it is not advisable when children are involved...(and) are best left to an attorney who is fully familiar with such cases." (p.175)

own two feet, without being dependent, for a change, on a third party, whether it be in the form of a spouse or one who goes by the name "lawyer"!

FOURTH ADVANTAGE: ***You Get To Make The Major Decisions On Your Own Life Yourself***
In theory, if you hired a lawyer, part of the service you are supposed to get from him or her is help with making decisions about your affairs. They are practically all-knowing, the theory goes, and they know which things have to be decided and the general standards and rules by which things are done in the courts. Or, at least, they are supposed to know!

However, by doing it yourself (and learning the court procedures and using the help provided you by this manual), you shall have **YOURSELF** known a lot about what needs doing and the way things are done generally in cases such as you may have. You will be the one that makes your own decision or settlement on your marital matters -- the so-called "collateral" and "ancillary" issues — based on YOUR OWN knowledge and on YOUR OWN best self-interest! You won't now have to depend on someone else, some "expert", to do that for you!!

F. The Major Collateral Or Marital Issues That Must Be Decided:

- that the marriage should be ended;
- how to divide any property and bills that you may have accumulated during the marriage; and
- whether there is to be spousal financial support, and if so for whom and how much.
  Where there are no minor children, that's just about all there is to it.

If you have children, you must also decide:

- who is to have custody of the children;
- how visitation is to be arranged; and
- how much is to be paid by whom for child support.
  (See Chapter 3, (pp. 13-28) for detailed discussion of collateral and ancillary issues in divorce).

As a practical matter, this is what the overwhelming majority of marital settlement agreements and divorce (dissolution of marriage) cases is basically all about — settling the practical affairs of the couple and watching out for the well-being of the minor children, if applicable. These are the things you must decide about in order to get a separation or divorce. If your spouse is in the picture and actively cares about what happens in the divorce, then you must be able either to talk over the issues with your spouse and come to some agreements, or you must be sure that your spouse in not likely to get a lawyer and actively oppose the divorce action.

G. You Should Try To Have Either An "Agreed" Or A "Default" Divorce

When a separation arises, or a divorce or dissolution lawsuit is filed, it raises the issues outlined above. These issues can be resolved in one of only three ways:

1) by ***"agreement"*** of the parties; or
2) by ***"default"*** of the other spouse, or
3) by ***"contest;"*** one spouse against the other.

In the "AGREED" case, the parties get together and settle the issues themselves and then, in effect, submit their agreement to court for its approval. In the "DEFAULT" situation, the respondent (the defendant-spouse) is properly notified of the fact that a lawsuit for divorce has been filed, but he does nothing about it, hence, as far as the court is concerned, no-response or opposition is deemed to have been filed by the defendant in that case, and hence, the Petitioner-spouse (the plaintiff) is awarded the divorce "BY DEFAULT" — that is, by the failure of the other spouse to show up to object to or contest the divorce case. In the third situation, the "CONTESTED" case, the respondent-spouse, usually through a lawyer, files a Response to the divorce action and comes to oppose and do battle with you in court. (It will usually be a more difficult task, though by no means an impossible one, for you to do your own divorce under this last (the "CONTESTED") category.

1. The "Default" Situation

In this kind of situation, the divorce is easy to do, providing you can only get the papers "served" on (i.e., properly delivered to) your spouse. After a short wait following the service of the divorce papers on your spouse, you just go ahead and file the rest of the divorce papers with the court and get your judgment. Even if your spouse is angry and unsupportive of the divorce action, it's considered that so long as no actual, formal "Answer" or Response is filed by him, there is no legal hindrance, and hence in official terms what he may otherwise be feeling means nothing — with respect to the divorce action.

2. The "Agreed" Divorce Situation

If your spouse is in the picture and actively cares about what happens, then it is extremely advisable that you should make efforts to reach an agreement with him (her) on the "collateral" or "ancillary" issues that are involved in your marriage (property division, child or spousal support, child visitation or custody, and the like).

Here are some of the many things you stand to gain by having an agreement or understanding with your spouse, whether in an oral, or, preferably, in a written form, in **advance** of your going through with your divorce:

I) It is much easier getting the divorce, especially since you won't have to chase your spouse around to have the papers served on him. This makes it faster, and a little cheaper, too.

II) It is more certain as to how the Court will likely decide matters in the end. The judge will very likely follow or adopt the terms of any agreement you and your spouse shall have had, providing such terms are not obviously unfair.

III) It will help the "defendant" or "respondent" spouse feel better about letting the divorce go through without contesting or having to hire a lawyer to "represent" him, since the terms of the Divorce Judgment (the final order) from the court would have been pretty much settled between you and him ahead of time.

IV) It invariably leads to better relations with your ex-spouse. Where there are children, this is extremely important.

In a word, the "agreed" type of divorce simply has so many big advantages that if at all there is any chance of working things out with your spouse, you should struggle for it long and hard! It's worth the try and effort.

H. Avoiding A "Contested" Divorce, Separation Or Settlement Case

Whether it is a divorce or separation, to fight, or not to fight , say the experts, is the point that divides the "easy" cases from the "hard" ones. The main reason, experts say, for a difficult time with a divorce situation, for example, is that such couples want to fight, or that they just can't keep from it! Such people are angry or hurt and want to hurt back. They want to use the law as a weapon, to revenge or force their spouse into some sort of response. The law, however, rarely has this result. Instead, what usually happens is that "the law" and the legal system almost always turn a **contested** divorce into a very unpleasant and very expensive failure. The divorce will still always go through in the end, but no one will be happy about it. What a cruel hoax! NO ONE EVER REALLY "WINS" IN A DIVORCE COURT BATTLE!!

Hence, if your case may turn into a fight, remember this: ***It is one thing to get a court order against someone, but it is very much another thing to be able to enforce that order.*** Especially in cases where there are children, a divorce is not a final solution since you have to deal with each other in the future because of the kids. In more ways than one, it really pays to work things out.

Whatever You Do, Please Avoid Ever Involving An Attorney!

Can You get a "friendly" separation or divorce (not to talk of a simple or affordable one!), once you and/or your spouse hire a lawyer and involve him in the process? **NO! YOU JUST DON'T STAND MUCH OF A CHANCE!!** It's too late already by then. Here's how a Chicago practicing divorce attorney and author summed up the reality:

> "Perhaps you have been making a valiant attempt to avoid hostility and deal fairly with each other in resolving property and parenting issues. Enter the lawyers. All that is over now. After all, this is an adversary proceeding; each side must be represented by different lawyers...Step back three paces — Draw!
>
> ***Now the contest has only begun. But there will be no winner among the parties... Except for the lawyers...The longer the contest, the greater their share of the spoils.***
>
> Are there alternatives to that scenario? Yes! One is to sit down together [with your spouse] and hash out your differences so that you can come up with an agreement. Then you can either handle your own divorce or present the substance to your respective lawyer...
>
> The second alternative is to go to a divorce mediation service...that helps the two parties come to their own voluntary agreement about disputed issues..."[5]

Try Working Things Out With Your Spouse

If you can't agree about basic things peacefully, maybe you should let some time pass. This is one strategy suggested by many experts. Wait to see if things settle down. It may probably help if you order another copy of this divorce/separation manual and send it to your spouse, and then try to discuss various sections of it with him or her directly — i.e., with no lawyer being involved on either side.

This is a good idea because your spouse may misunderstand what a divorce (dissolution of marriage) is all about, or what exactly you are seeking by the divorce action, and informed people are usually less emotional and irrational. It can get the two of you talking about practical, constructive things.

Also, this manual, especially the informational material contained in this chapter, can help to drive the following points across to your spouse:

- Fighting will not automatically prevent the divorce, it will only make it more unpleasant and much more time consuming and expensive — to BOTH parties.
- Even contested dissolutions are decided according to the standards discussed in this manual. Any monetary advantage gained by a court fight is usually wiped out by the legal fees and other costs of the battle. How much price tag do you place on the emotional strain and future relations with your spouse and children, for example?

If the reason you can't agree is emotional, or a basic inability to communicate, you can still be very successful if you can both agree to involve a third person. A trusted friend, a priest, a rabbi, a member of the clergy, or a professional mediator or counselor (but, please no lawyers!) can often be very helpful at getting things worked out.

Listen to the wise words of ***Sandra Kalenik***, an experienced, long-term Washington D.C. area author and expert on divorce matters:

> "Over the years I have talked with many divorce lawyers, mediators, and people involved in the divorce process. If there is one common problem divorcing people have, it is that they are emotional and often do not think clearly about what they are doing. Many are extremely angry, and revenge against their spouse pops up as the only answer to their problems. They allow revenge to replace cogent thinking. When this happens, bad decisions often result to the detriment of both parties...

---

[5] Nancy E. Albert, writing in "Insider's Guide To Divorce In Illinois: The Practical Consumer Divorce Manual", at p.11. Another experienced divorce lawyer, Burton I. Monasch, past President of the New York Chapter of the American Academy of Matrimonial Lawyers, has this to say: "...the courts are the last place a person resolving a matrimonial dispute should be...Because of the adversary nature of the law, an atmosphere of heat and ill-will is immediately created...I believe that the day a matrimonial problem gets in the hands of lawyers the individuals are in deep trouble." Monasch in Marriage and Divorce Today, a New York City bi-weekly newsletter, December 19, 1977.

If I were to offer advice, it would be this: stay as calm and unemotional as you possibly can. Learn what your rights are, decide what you need and want, and keep as cool as possible. When you are feeling depressed, overwhelmed, spiteful, or furious, talk it over with a respected friend, therapist, or member of the clergy...***Whatever you do, try not to act out your emotions by making them a legal battlefield among you, your spouse, and any children you might have. Unless you are very wealthy and wish to transfer a good chunk of that wealth to your attorney's coffers, don't argue over everything.*** Be selective with your fights. This detachment can save you more later than you might be able to realize now. "[6] (Emphasis added by present writer)

I. If Direct Negotiations Doesn't Work, Use Mediation

But, even if all efforts at direct-negotiations between you and your spouse (or cohabiting partner) have been exhausted and they are unsuccessful, or such negotiations are not feasible, all is still not lost yet. Far from it! In fact, quite to the contrary, fortunately there is a new potent devise that has increasingly gained approval with the courts and popularity among divorcing and separating couples across the country. Such device can come to your rescue. It's called: MEDIATION.

Mediation basically involves using the assistance and services of a professional negotiator, called a "mediator", to help couples negotiate their agreement or settlement. Often, the mediator is a social worker, or even a lawyer, but well trained specifically in the art of family conflict negotiations and resolution. In recent times private mediation services and centers have sprung up across the country, their specialty being mediating divorce and separation cases — including property settlement, and child custody and support arrangements, alimony, etc.

Perhaps not surprising, at the beginning divorce lawyers have been among the major detractors of mediation as the lawyers claim that, because mediators are often not lawyers, their services often fail (they claim) to protect the right of either party in that mediators, the lawyers contend, are sometimes unaware of the legal ramifications of their decisions. Nevertheless, mediation has gained increasing popularity with the public who are aware of and educated about it.

The chief attraction of mediation which has accounted for its growing popularity especially among upper middle-class and wealthier persons (but not necessarily among divorce lawyers!), are two-fold: first, unlike "arbitration" (negotiation arrangement in which the parties must abide by the decision of the arbitrator), mediators are involved in the process only to facilitate agreement by offering objective, professional, third-party alternatives acceptable to both sides; and secondly, use of mediation have been noted to save the parties both substantial time and money relative to the traditional method of using the lawyer-dominated settlement arrangements, and often includes in one flat fee package the cost of preparing and filing the necessary written agreements and court papers to finalize the separation or divorce judicially.

Use County Counseling Services, If Possible

In addition to privately-run mediation, many counties in certain states across the country (e.g., Arizona, Washington, Oregon, Wisconsin, New Hampshire, New Mexico, etc., to name just a few) now have a Conciliation Court or unit thereof, which provides marriage counseling for troubled marriages, either before or during a divorce action. They would help you save your marriage if and when there's still any hope, but when it's too late and hopeless they can also help you dissolve it on a more peaceful and civilized basis. Conferences with the counselors are often free or at a nominal fee, and their confidentiality is usually protected by law, so all you can lose is time. You can first try it. And if, in the end, you don't like their services, you can always go back to your legal proceeding and pursue your divorce or separation accordingly.

J. Putting It All In A Written Agreement

If you and your spouse can agree on working out things between yourselves and having an "agreed" divorce (or separation), one usual way of simplifying matters is to put it all (the terms of your understandings) in writing. That's where the drawing up of an appropriate settlement or separation agreement (or other types), the primary subject matter

---

[6] Sandra Kalenik, in How To Get A Divorce, (Washington Book Trading Company, 1991) pp. x-xi

of this guidebook, comes into play — and handily. (See Chapter 6 for the actual drafting procedures for such agreements). As is more elaborately covered elsewhere in the manual (See Section E of Chapter 4 at pp. 31-3), in these contemporary times written separation/settlement agreements between couples have become the basic instrument of effectuating peaceful, compatible divorce or breakups, accepted and encouraged by the courts. In a word, once a good written separation or settlement agreement is drawn up, if an action for a divorce were later to be filed by either party (or by both), the divorce action will almost automatically be resolved in accordance with the provisions of the written agreement, thereby leading to a far more amicable "uncontested" case in which at the final hearing only one spouse need attend. The court, in effect, will basically review and approve the agreement you and your spouse had reached and, providing the terms are half way fair, incorporate it into the divorce DECREE to grant you your divorce. (Or, in very rare occasions, it may require changes in the agreement before approving it and granting the divorce in a situation where, for example, it finds the agreement to be too one-sided or grossly unfair).

How To Do It

Hence, the message? It's simple: that you had better tried and at least exerted some efforts, and if at all it's all possible, by all means work out a written agreement with your spouse, anyway. If you try your darnest but in the end you and your spouse still cannot agree on signing one, well that's too bad; you can still proceed without one then. (The procedures for the actual drafting of agreements are in Chapters 6.)

CHAPTER 3

THE TYPICAL PROPERTY AND OTHER "COLLATERAL" ISSUES YOU AND YOUR SPOUSE OR PARTNER MAY HAVE TO WORK OUT BETWEEN YOU

1. THE MOST IMPORTANT THING: TRY REACHING AN UNDERSTANDING OR SETTLEMENT AGREEMENT WITH YOUR SPOUSE OR PARTNER

For the vast majority of American couples, the issues you and your spouse or partner are to settle during (or, preferably, before) a divorce proceeding or separation or settlement agreement, would probably include one or more of these: property division, child custody, child support, visitation rights, alimony, division of marital debts and bills, settlement of life or health insurance benefits or retirement funds, etc.

A word of wisdom: if some of these items are applicable to you, it would generally be most helpful for you as a do-it-yourselfer, if you can reach an amicable understanding with your spouse about them. This way, you would be in a position to file under the far-easier, and more desired **"uncontested"** divorce or settlement procedures. In general, the court is likely to grant whatever terms an adult husband and wife couple freely agrees to, providing that what is agreed to are legal and pretty fair, and not unconscionable or harmful to one party, especially to the welfare of the minor children, if applicable.

Therefore, as a general principle, the key to getting, say, a fair—and uncontested—property division in a divorce or settlement situation (when there is any property to speak of, in the first place), or a fair child support or maintenance term, is really for both spouses to speak with each other and learn to practice some art of marital comprising and generosity. It's that simple!

2. SETTLING THE DIFFERENT ISSUES WITH YOUR SPOUSE OR PARTNER

Let's go into the collateral (they're also called "ancillary" or "incidental") questions in divorce in a little more detail. ***The following issues will be discussed:***

A. Property Division
B. Settlement of Insurance Pension & Retirement Funds,* Stock-Option/Profit-Sharing Plans, Social Security Benefits, Etc.
C. Division of Marital Debts & Bills
D. Alimony (Maintenance)
E. Custody of Children, if Applicable
F. Visitation Rights With Children
G. Child Support (if Applicable)
H. Other Issues

A. PROPERTY DIVISION

In a nutshell, the legal principles by which marital property is divided or allocated upon divorce, fall under three basic categories under various states' rules:

i) **The "Community Property" States.** Here, in such states,the spouses split ***equally*** all property acquired by either or both parties DURING the marriage, generally excluding, as each spouse's "separate property," those acquired by them either before the marriage or by gift or inheritance.

ii) **"Equitable Distribution" Property States.** Here, in such states marital property acquired or owned by the spouses during the marriage is distributable to them on the basis of what is just and fair, with each couple's circumstances determined on a case-by-case manner.[1]

In general, the separate property which a spouse owned PRIOR to marriage and any property which a spouse receives by gift or inherits (either before or during the marriage), is usually treated as his/her own "separate property" not subject to division in most equitable distribution states, and only any other property (including any income from such separate property that was earned during the marriage) is distributable. However, in a few states (Alaska, Connecticut, Georgia, Hawaii, Indiana, Kansas Massachusetts, Michigan, Montana, New Hampshire, North Dakota, Oregon, South Dakota, Utah, Vermont, and Wyoming), ALL of the spouses' property is subject to being divided on an equitable basis, regardless of when or how it was acquired or held, including any gifts and inheritances — providing the court feels it's just and proper to do so.[2]

iii) **"Common Law" or "Title" Property States.** Here, the ownership of individual property is allocated to the respective spouses according to who has legal title to it or who had his/her name on it at the time of the divorce.

Almost all of the states, in deed except for Mississippi, which is a "title" state, are today either community property or equitable distribution-based. Among these, nine states are "community property" states: Arizona, California, Idaho, Louisiana, Nevada, New Mexico, Texas, Washington, and Wisconsin.

NOTE: Rather fortunately for us, though, as a practical matter it turns out that most couples don't really have to worry about the problem of "property division" in the first place, since in the first place, they either have no major property to fuss over, or they've already given up all there is to one or the other spouse even long before they decide it's time to file for divorce. Hence, for most couples seeking divorce , this issue will probably be an irrelevant one, anyway! Furthermore, bear in mind that, again, as a practical matter, the issue of what state law or what method of property division to apply will only arise where the judge has to come into the picture to rule on it because the spouses themselves are not able (or willing to come to agreement on their own regarding the way to divide up their property.

The point to remember is that these rules are, in the final analysis, only guidelines and 'talking points' for negotiating and discussion; if you and your spouse can mutually agree on dividing up your property in any manner or proportion, that division, even if only halfway fair and reasonable, will be just as valid and sufficient for all intents and purposes!

Who Should Have The Family House?

For most couples, a home is often the most important and most expensive acquisition they ever made, and "partitioning" (dividing up) of a house is not easily acceptable to either spouse. Fortunately, as a practical matter, in the majority of cases the spouse who does not have custody of the children (usually the husband) will usually agree to

---

[1] New York's Equitable Distribution Bill of 1980 is typical of equitable property division states. It treats marriage as an "economic partnership" for which the property accumulated by it at the time of it's dissolution is to be distributed to the partners (the spouses) on an "equitable" basis — i.e., on a fair basis, although not necessarily 50-50. The law states that, except for couples who settle peacefully without contest, or have privately entered into a written "opting-out agreement" setting out how marital property is to be divided up in the event of a divorce, marital property (defined as "all property acquired by either or both spouses during the marriage") is to be distributed upon divorce by the court "equitably between the parties, considering the circumstances of the case and of the respective parties."

[2] Included among the group which divide marital property "equitably," are the following territories: the District of Columbia, Puerto Rico and The Virgin Islands.

an arrangement whereby the other spouse may have the use of the house in the interest of the proper rearing of the children or, he will frequently agree to deed his interest in the property to the spouse when the equity in the house (the current market value of the house, minus the outstanding mortgage on it) isn't large.

But what if you and your spouse can't agree on anything, by what principles do you (or, does the court) decide who is to have the house? There are a few options, the more common solutions, you can consider:

- Put the house (or apartment) up for sale and divide its "net" proceeds, if any (the balance from the sales proceeds, if any, after subtracting the mortgage on it, and the estate taxes, commission, etc.). This method, by the way, is the simplest way. Or,

- One spouse, especially the one who does not have custody of the children in a marriage involving minor children, may grant the other spouse the right to "exclusive use and possession" of the marital house for a specified number of years, say, until she remarries or the youngest child attains the age of 18 or 21, without actually giving her the ownership, at which time the house would be sold and the net profits shared equally. Or,

- One spouse may simply agree to buy the other's share in the house — i.e., he or she is allowed to retain possession of the home, with the title to the house transferred to her at divorce, while she either takes out a second mortgage to pay off the house to the other spouse or gives the other spouse a note to pay him off either installmentally or upon the sale of the house or the attainment of a designated age by the last child. Or,

- One spouse, the one not having the pension plan (say the wife), may balance the house against the other spouse's (the husband's) pension; the wife simply receives full title to the house in return for waiving all rights to her husband's pension.

NOTE: One "sticky" issue that often arises in relation to how to apportion a house, has to do with the down payment on the house when it was bought. One spouse, for example, might have made the down payment out of his or her own separate resources — that is, money which was neither part of the community property (if they lived in a community property state) nor part of the marital property. Subsequently, however, all mortgage payments were paid out of marital funds. Thereupon, at the time of separation or divorce it is legitimate to have the down payment amount written into the settlement agreement or divorce judgment stipulating that he or she will receive that amount up front, before the final split is made (assuming it's a community property state), and any appreciation divided up.

B. SETTLEMENT OF INSURANCE, PENSION & RETIREMENT FUNDS.[3] STOCK-OPTION/PROFIT-SHARING PLANS, SOCIAL SECURITY BENEFITS, ETC.

a) Insurance Funds: In a marital dissolution where either or both spouses maintain some retirement or insurance policies (e.g., life insurance, health insurance, pension right, etc.), it is not unusual to find that one spouse may have named the other as the beneficiary of the proceeds. One thing the spouses should remember to discuss — and arrive at an agreement on — in such situations, is who should retain or give up which beneficiary rights in which policy or funds? Couples may also agree on maintaining a medical or life insurance policy for the benefit of the children, where applicable, and how it should be paid for and by whom.

[3] Common among retirement plans, are the following: Individual Retirement Accounts (IRA's); IRS 401 (K) Retirement Plans; HR-10 Retirement Plans (KEOGH'S): Self-Employment Person's Individual Retirement Accounts (SEP-IRA's); Tax Sheltered Annuities (TSA's) and Employee Stock options (ESOP's).

b) Pension & Retirement Plans: In the last several decades, pensions have become one of a couples' largest marital assets, and almost every state now considers the value of benefits from retirement and pension plans, and from stock options and profit-sharing plans during the course of a marriage, as part of a spouse's assets or marital property subject to sharing upon divorce. Consequently, figuring out how to value such plans and to divide them equally is important in divorce or separation settlements. The issue can be a thorny one.

Assuming that your spouse has an employment which has a pension plan (only 76.1 million Americans or just 46% of all American workers, for example, were covered by pension plan in 1990), an important question is: how do you evaluate the pension and divide it in a divorce settlement? Here are a few options that can be considered:

Option #1: Other assets could be given to the nonpensioned spouse in lieu of a 100% right to the pension. The way this works is this: you let the pensioned spouse (the covered employee) keep the pension benefits and give the other spouse cash or other assets worth half the current value of that part of the benefits accrued during the marriage. (But this, however, requires that you be able to figure out what the current value of the benefits are, meaning basically that you'd need the services of an insurance actuary). In other words, let's say the parties jointly own a house, the employee spouse (the one with the pension) keeps his or her full pension but waives his rights to the house, and in return, the non-pensioned spouse receives full title to the house but also waives all her rights to the pension.

Or, as another example, one spouse, say the husband, may retain his entire interest in his retirement fund by giving up to his wife his one-half interest in a jointly held bank account with his wife, or by giving his car which he wholly owns, to his wife in return. Trade off arrangements are generally preferred among couples because retirement plans are often very difficult to divide up without terminating it and cashing it in. Hence, often it is customary to give other assets to the non-pensioned spouse in lieu of a right in the pension as it usually saves everyone a whole lot of headaches.

Basically, you'll have to hire an actuary (a pension or insurance evaluation specialist), since the calculations involved are usually very complicated even for lawyers and other experts, who'll employ the proper methods to substitute the present value of the unemployed spouse's share of the pension with other marital property, and thereby place a present value on the pension. And, with that figure, the pension can then be divided equitably, as agreed to between the spouses. [To get an actuary to appraise the value for you, just look under "actuaries" and "insurance consultants" in your local Yellow Pages].

If the parties are living, for example, in a "community property" state, the pension rights will be treated as an asset to be split 50-50 at its calculated, present value; and if living in an "equitable distribution" state, the pension rights will be treated as an asset to be split in other "equitable" proportions as agreed to by the spouses.

Option #2: The pension may be allocated to the non-employee spouse based upon the ratio of years the employee-spouse worked during the marriage and his/her total years of employment. (Example: husband worked five years prior to marrying wife, and fifteen years during the marriage, during which time they lived in a community property state before they divorce. This means that the wife will be entitled to share in only three-quarters (i.e., 15 years of marriage out of 20 years of work) of the pension, and she should look to split that three-quarters share 50-50 being that they live in a community property state. [With this method, though, the non-employee spouse may not collect until the employee spouse actually retires, and who knows, he may die or lose the job in the meantime before retirement, or the pension fund may go bankrupt, in each case the non-pension spouse would be left without any recovery.]

Option #3: The value of the employee spouse's anticipated pension could be treated as a future asset in which the other spouse (the non-employee spouse) could have some share. You'll give, in other words, the non-employee spouse the right to receive part of the retirement benefits when those benefits are eventually paid out.

Qualified Domestic Relations Order (QDRO)

Under the above third option, it is not necessary to figure out the current value of the benefits; both spouses will simply have to wait to receive any payments until the employee-spouse is eligible to receive the benefits. HOWEVER, HERE'S AN IMPORTANT POINT: if you choose this option, your settlement agreement with your spouse must generally contain a provision for what is known as a "Qualified Domestic Relations Order" (QDRO) as applicable under retirement plan rules. Furthermore, your settlement agreement, along with the final decree of dissolution of marriage, must be filed with, and be accepted by, the administrator of the retirement plan involved before it will be effective.

A Qualified Domestic Relations Order, or simply QDRO, is a court-signed Order which, if and when it gets signed at the time of a divorce, authorizes the administrator of the pension plan to "qualify" (comply with) the stipulations of the order — that is, for it to make certain that the plan meets certain requirements which principally ensures that the pension assets are split according to the couple's agreement.

Note, though, that QDRO orders apply ONLY to pension plans of two type — the "defined benefits" and "defined contributions" types, such as 401(K) and profit-sharing plans. They do not apply to Individual Retirement Accounts (IRA) or to special arrangements that companies set up for high-paid executives. For more on QDRO and its procedures, see Appendix B.

Whatever the method of sharing the pension that applies, it should be emphasized, however, that unless you have been married for a fairly long time, the value of the retirement plan (and of your share of it) may be insignificant and not worth the trouble. Furthermore, as stated above, surely it's true that nowadays there's generally no disputing the fact that benefits from pension or retirement plans, or from stock option or profit sharing plans which are earned during the marriage, are legitimately classifiable as assets which could be subject to sharing by the other spouse upon a divorce. *But where the problem arises on this issue, however, is with respect to determining what the actual* PRESENT VALUE *of these items is—in particular, the current value of the benefits that accrued (the amount of money that was contributed) during the marriage.* On your part, here's the simple advice to follow: simply ask the employer or administrator of the plan (or an insurance actuary, or accountant or CPA) for help with working out this information.

What about social security benefits, or military and federal pensions and benefits? With respect to social security, under the law any benefits received by a spouse are not classifiable as marital property or subject to division upon divorce, the rule being that these are federal benefits and are not subject to state laws. Paradoxically, though, on the other hand military retirement pensions and federal civil annuity benefits, though federally administered, are in most states subject to division upon divorce, especially for marriages of long duration (generally over 10 years).

C. DIVISION OF MARITAL DEBTS AND BILLS

Whichever ways the parties voluntarily agree to divide up the debts they jointly signed or co-signed for between them will ordinarily be acceptable to the court. Generally, only debts and obligations incurred by the parties DURING their marriage are applicable, and any such obligation incurred prior to the marriage are deemed a "separate" obligation for which the spouse who incurred them is solely liable. Just to make sure, however, include **ALL** of the debts that are outstanding and that legitimately apply. More importantly, make sure that you promptly take away those charge cards or joint check books from each other and destroy them. That way, you prevent the possibility of finding that there are more debts for you later!

In those states which fall under the equitable property principle of property ownership (see p.14), the marital debts are to be divided "equitably," as reasonably seen fit by the couple; and for those who fall under the community property states (p.14), the community debts are split 50-50, unless otherwise agreed to by mutual consent.

D. ALIMONY (MAINTENANCE)

Alimony, (it's now more commonly referred to also as "maintenance" or "spousal support" in some states) is, of course, the term given to court-ordered allowance a husband (or wife) pays to his wife (or husband) for her separate maintenance after divorce, Nowadays, in the wake of the women's liberation movement, the trend among most divorcing women is to refuse to demand alimony payments from their husbands, and even when they ask for it, the judges are no longer quite as willing to grant it, any way. Furthermore, in the present era, alimony is no longer the sole or exclusive right of the wife, as it once was in the past. Today, the husband is just as eligible to apply for — and to be awarded — alimony from the courts under the laws of most states, as the basis for spousal support has dramatically shifted from the sex of the spouse to the need of the spouse. If, however, a separation or settlement agreement between the spouses had called for the payment of alimony, the judge, viewing the agreement essentially as a separate contract, might generally enforce the provision.[4]

Also, you should note that generally award of alimony is not commonly made, either. According to one estimate, only in approximately 15 percent of all divorces are alimony or spousal support of any kind made or even considered necessary or applicable. And the length of time during which alimony payments are paid after divorce has also been decreasing in recent times; it now runs an average of 2 to 5 years. And such payments, for the specific duration they are fixed to be made, is designed specifically for one purposes, namely, for "rehabilitation" — that is, to allow the recipient (dependent) spouse just that limited time he/she needs to get himself/herself self-supporting.[6]

The important question that often arises when alimony is paid at all, is: what amount of alimony should be asked or paid? There is no set amount that is applicable for all cases. As one informed analyst, a lawyer, put it, "The dominant rule in the United States is that such an award rests in the discretion of the court. Basically, alimony depends on the spouse's needs and conduct, and the other spouse's ability to pay."[5]

All that is safe to say is that any amount the husband can afford, and to which his spouse can readily agree, would probably receive the signature of approval by the judge. And, indeed, even in situations where the states have established, by law, guidelines for awarding alimony, the decision by the court as to when to approve or order such an award, or the amount of the award, or as to the spouse who should make the alimony payment, will still have to be determined by consideration of certain criteria, such as these: the standard of living of the parties, their relative income, their assets and obligations, the earning ability and prospects of each spouse, the length of the marriage, the needs of each of the parties and of their children, the occupation and vocational skills of each spouse, the employability of each , the age and health of the parties and of their children, and what other responsibility each party may have for the support of other persons, such as the couple's minor children or children from a previous marriage, etc.

The two most important considerations among judges seem to be the length of the marriage and the earning abilities of the spouses. In general, alimony award has the best chance of being favorably ruled on and approved where there had been a long marriage, particularly if one spouse earns considerably more than the other, or one spouse earns all the income and the other earns practically no income while, say, having to raise the couple's children. Alimony is not favored much, on the other hand, where the marriage is relatively short or very short, or where there are no minor children and both spouses are healthy and relatively young and can presumably take care of themselves.

You should note, though, that as a practical reality, compared to child support, spousal support (alimony) has a lower priority to child support in divorce proceedings. The reason this is so is related to several practical reasons. For one thing, in many families, once adequate child support payment is made, there often isn't much left over for more than token spousal support to be attempted; secondly, alimony is deemed to concern grown adults who, presumably, can cater for themselves far better than the minor children of a marriage.

---

[4] Note: Note that alimony payments (providing it is based either on a written agreement or a court order) is tax-deductible to the payer, while the recipient, on the other hand, is required to report it as taxable income to herself. Child support payments, on the other hand, is not taxable to the recipient.

[5] Here's how one recent report summed up the prevailing state of affairs: "With the exception of marriages that have lasted 20 years or more, in which one spouse has no employment skills or is physically or mentally unable to enter the work force, the concept of long-term alimony has generally become a thing of the past. Instead, the courts now more frequently provide dependent spouse with short-term payments that, at most last for five to seven years and never longer than the duration of the marriage (from our experience, the average is somewhere between three and five years).... During this period, the dependent spouse, who in almost every case is the woman, is expected to acquire skills so that she may enter the work force and eventually earn her own living. In other words, the law is now written to avoid placing a permanent responsibility [of support on] a divorced spouse indefinitely." (Koff, *Love and the Law*, Simon & Schuster, N.Y., 1989, p.192)

[6] Edward Siegel, How to Avoid Lawyers. Ballantine Books, New York 1989 p. 125

If a spouse is the 'guilty' party or the party who's 'at fault' in a divorce, does that affect the alimony award? It depends. Not every misbehavior will disqualify a spouse, but serious offenses, such as adultery, or an attempt on the spouse's life, might still bar a spouse from receiving alimony or at least affect the amount or duration of the award. A growing number of states, however, (29 of them) now award alimony without regard to marital misconduct.

States in which marital misconduct is either considered or is a bar to alimony (21 states plus District of Columbia and Puerto Rico):

Alabama, Connecticut, District of Columbia, Florida, Georgia, Idaho, Kentucky, Louisiana, Massachusetts, Michigan, Missouri, New Hampshire, North Carolina, North Dakota, Pennsylvania, Rhode Island, South Carolina, South Dakota, Tennessee, Virginia, West Virginia and Puerto Rico.

States in which marital misconduct is not considered (29 states and the Virgin Islands):

Alaska, Arizona, Arkansas, California, Colorado, Delaware, Hawaii, Illinois, Indiana, Iowa, Kansas, Maine, Maryland, Massachusetts, Minnesota, Mississippi, Montana, Nebraska, Nevada, New Jersey, New Mexico, New York, Ohio, Oklahoma, Oregon, Vermont, Washington, Wisconsin, Wyoming and the Virgin Islands.

One way of gauging how much alimony a given spouse should pay in a given situation is by gauging what proportion of his income should reasonably be granted to the receiving spouse as alimony. Determination of that figure will be based on a number of factors: how much the paying spouse makes, what assets he has, the social status of the parties, the standard of living the parties have been accustomed to, and, not the least of all, the amount of child support he also has to pay. One analyst ventures a 'rule of thumb' of combined alimony and child support of between 15% and 50% of the man's pay, but adds that "more commonly, the average would probably be from 20% to 40%, although there necessarily is a wide variation, based on the individual case."[7]
Furthermore, many states now make use of a chart that offers a standard spousal (alimony) as well as child support figure, which sets forth the minimum, average and maximum amounts per week or month. Upon working out the figures on such a chart, the judge merely decides on the amount to be awarded based on the individual case. [Ask your court clerk for a copy of your state's alimony/child support chart.]

When alimony is applicable, however, parties had better make sure of the following: 1) that the **exact** amount of alimony to be paid is specified in the documents in **periodic** terms (weekly, bi-weekly, semi-monthly or monthly);[8] 2) that alimony payments are not lumped together with, but are stated separately from, child support payments, if applicable; and 3) that the time at which the alimony payments are to terminate is expressly specified (e.g., whether it should be at the death of the husband, remarriage by the wife, graduation from a trade or profession, etc.)

E. CUSTODY OF THE CHILDREN, IF APPLICABLE

Ordinarily, by and large, the courts tend to award the "sole" custody of the children to the mother almost automatically, unless it can be adequately shown that she is an "unfit" mother (usually meaning there's and immoral or criminal habit in her past or lifestyle which she is likely to transmit to the child.) This policy is based on the so-called "tender years doctrine" traditional thinking (which is probably valid in most instances) that holds that mothers are generally better at caring for babies than are the average fathers. ***As a general rule, however, any child custody arrangements the plaintiff is able to present to the court which is mutually agreed to by the spouses, if half-way reasonable, would usually be respected and approved by the judge.***

---

[7] Siegel, Ibid. p.126

[8] The need for this is essentially to avoid being trapped in all of the "tax consequence" complications that might arise. For a fuller treatment of the tax ramifications of property division in marital situations, See Chapter 12.

The overwhelming majority of states now permit a form of custody arrangement that is known as ***"joint custody"*** allowing the both parents together to have a shared legal custody of the child and equal voice in the major decisions involved in the raising of the child. In deed, as of this writing only 6 states, and the District of Columbia — Georgia, North Dakota, Rhode Island, South Carolina, Virginia, and Wyoming — do not specifically authorize or provide for a joint custody form of custody under their state law.

If your state's laws permit a joint custody system, and you and your spouse want this to apply in your written agreement and divorce, then you must so stipulate in your divorce petition or complaint, and, more importantly, you must be prepared at the time of divorce to provide the court with some information and explanation (it's called a **"parenting plan"**) as to why the judge can expect that you and your spouse will now exhibit, *as parents*, the kind of maturity and mutual cooperation that you never showed *as spouses*, so as to be able to convince the judge that you can BOTH make such a joint custody arrangement workable and practicable. Joint custody permits both parents to take turns keeping the children, if the parents so decide, and then to have the usual right and responsibility to jointly make major decisions concerning the child(ren). *Currently, however, the trend regarding the matter seems to be strongly in favor of joint custody arrangements, as it is increasingly viewed by many in and out of the judicial system as a desirable way of encouraging greater contact of the child with BOTH parents, which is generally believed to be in the child's best interest.*

Other states, very few in number, also permit a third form of custody called **"divided" or "alternating" custody**, whereby each parent will exercise custody of the child for alternating periods of time, say six months out of a year, or for every other month or week.

And, on the vital question of who between the spouses should have custody, how do you make that determination? By what criteria? One recent analyst gives this informative but enthusiastic summary of the "commonsense" standard now being generally employed by the courts in making such a decision:

> "The most recent trend in custody legislation and court decisions provides one of the most common-sense approaches to the problem. Increasingly, courts are looking at a child's day-to-day circumstances in an effort to determine which parent has been the primary caregiver of the child. The parent who has provided most of the day-to-day care for the child during the marriage is then considered to be the most likely candidate to continue on as the primary custodian of the child after the divorce. The preference is given to the parent which has actively participated in caring for the child and performed the majority of the parenting activities: preparing meals, readying the child for sleep, sharing in their playtime, dealing with medical problems, participating in their education, etc. This method does not presuppose that either parent has an entitlement to being awarded custody, but rather is based on an examination of the reality of the burdens of parenthood. The decision is based on the practical considerations of which parent has provided the most time, care, and guidance to the child prior to the actual divorce. It allows each parent an equal right to ***earn*** the custody of a child by providing care for the child before the divorce proceeding begins. This method of selection of the parent to have physical custody places the greatest emphasis on which [one of them] has been providing the most parental care for the child prior to the divorce. Selection of the primary care-giver as continuing custodian generally fosters a home life of stability and continuity for the child. In the family upheaval caused by divorce, this factor deserves considerable attention."[9]

F. A PARENT'S VISITATION RIGHTS WITH THE CHILDREN

Under most states' laws, one parent, usually the mother, gets custody of the children, while the other parent makes up for it by having the rights to visit with (or take out) the children on given days of the week or month. In general, it is not difficult to work out a reasonable visitation arrangement with the other spouse, once you let one overriding consideration be your guide: consideration of what is in the **child's** own best interest, and **NOT** of what is in the special interest of this or that parent. The facts about this are not in dispute: most child psychologists and experts are in complete

---

[9] **Daniel Sitarz,** *Divorce Yourself: The National No-Fault Divorce Kit,* **Nova Publishing Company, 1991, p.102**

agreement that the interest of the child is best served and maximized whenever he can get a "balanced piece" of **both** parents as much as practicable, whether in marriage or after divorce.

SAMPLE VISITATION GUIDELINES

The following is a sample of the type of Visitation Guidelines that some courts and counties are adopting. This sample is from Hamilton County of Ohio. Be sure to check with your local county Clerk of Court's office to determine if your county has adopted visitation guidelines for the non-custodial parent. In any event, you can always adapt some (or all) of these provisions for use in your own case, if agreeable, to draft your own visitation terms.

Note that you need not (no one couple needs to) pick any or all the terms specified here. You can pick and choose, and modify or expand on any terms as better preferred.

■ The non-custodial parent shall have visitation on *alternate* weekends from Friday at 6:00 p.m. to Sunday evening at 6:00 p.m.

■ The non-custodial parent shall have visitation from 5:30 p.m. to 8:30 p.m. on a weeknight *preceding* the weekends during which there is visitation.

■ During *even*-numbered years, the non-custodial parent shall have visitation on New Year's Day, President's Day, Memorial Day, Veteran's Day, and Thanksgiving. Each of these visitations shall begin at 10:00 a.m. and continue until 8:30 p.m.

■ The non-custodial parent shall be entitled to four weeks of additional visitation each year, this visitation may be exercised during the child's school break, at Christmas time, the child's break from school and summer visitation, or at any other appropriate time during the year.

■ During *odd* numbered years, the non-custodial parent shall have visitation on Martin Luther King Day, Easter, Fourth of July, and Labor Day. Each of these visitations shall begin at 10:00 a.m. and continue until 8:30 p.m.

■ On Mother's Day, the children shall be with the mother, and on Father's Day the children shall be with the father, no matter whose turn for visitation it is. Visitation shall begin at 10:00 a.m. and continue until 8:30 p.m.

■ During even numbered years, the non-custodial parent shall have visitation on the child's birthday. If the child's birthday falls on a non-school day, the visitation shall take place from 10:00 a.m. and continue until 8:30 p.m. If the child's birthday falls on a school day, visitation shall take place from 5:30 p.m. to 8:30 p.m.

■ The non-custodial parent shall not exercise visitation on holidays other than those which the non-custodial parent is entitled as described in the above paragraphs, except as otherwise agreed by the parties.

Note: The holiday schedule may be modified to accommodate the parties' religious preference

■ Make-up days shall be given if due to an emergency, the child or non-custodial parent cannot visit at the scheduled time or if the custodial parent denies visitation without just cause. All make-up days shall be rescheduled and exercised within thirty days.

■ Extended visitations are to be arranged within seven days from the time the parent's vacation schedules are posted by their employers. The non-custodial parent shall notify the custodial parent in writing of the time desired for extended visitation no later than 30 days prior to the requested extended visitation.

■ The children and/or custodial parent do not have to wait for the non-custodial parent to arrive for visitation more than 30 minutes. The non-custodial parent who is more than 30 minutes late for a particular visitation, shall forfeit that visitation.

■ The non-custodial parent who is more than 30 minutes late in returning the children without calling to make arrangements, shall, for just cause, be subject to contempt.

■ The custodial parent may not remove the children from the State of ________ and establish residence for them in another state without a Court order or an agreement signed by the parties.

■ In the event that the parties are unable to reach an agreement regarding transportation for visitation, *(Plaintiff/defendant)* shall provide transportation at commencement of the visitation period and ________ shall provide transportation at termination of the visitation period.

■ The custodial parent shall arrange for the appropriate school officials to release to the non-custodial parent any and all information concerning the children.

■ The custodial parent shall authorize the release of any and all medical information and records concerning the child to the non-custodial parent. In the event the child's illness requires medical attention by a physician, the custodial parent shall promptly notify the non-custodial parent. Elective surgery shall only be performed after consultation with the non-custodial parent.

■ Any child who is twelve years of age or older may set and determine visitation with the non-custodial parent.

NOTE: Willful non-compliance with the visitation order of the Court may result in a Finding of Contempt.

G. CHILD SUPPORT OBLIGATIONS (IF APPLICABLE)

Closely interrelated with the issue of child custody is the issue of child support. It is the legal obligation of parents, both the mother and father, but more so for the father, to provide adequate and continuous financial support for THEIR minor or infant children — that is, generally children under 18 years of age. Under most states' laws, though, it may extend to 21 years of age, where the child is provably in actual, *active* attendance at a school or college for that duration.

What is "adequate" support for a non-custodial parent to pay in a divorce situation? The rule is to determine what is adequate by the circumstances of the parents, as well as of the children, on a case-by-case basis. The factors considered are pretty much the same as those in an alimony case: The need of the children, the ability of the non-custodial parent (usually the father) to pay, etc. And even if the custodial parent has substantial capacity, the other parent is not relieved of his own obligation.

Some of the questions that would determine this, include: How much money does the father (or the mother, if there's no father) earn? Is the father a man of independent wealth, or not? Does he have other children he's supporting from a previous marriage? Is the child a normal child requiring no extraordinary expenditures, or is he, say, a diabetic who would require special care and extra expenditures, etc.?

One eminent analyst gives an estimate of the "fair" amount that the paying parent should pay for child support and alimony, combined, as some 20% to 40% of the paying parent's income "in the average case," depending on the section of the country, and the income and the living standards of the **couple.**[10] ***In any event, it should always be remembered that, in general, when the husband and wife can, on their own, agree on the amount of child support to be paid, there's not much of a problem and the court will usually go along. But it's only when they can't work out this matter (or agree on a figure) by themselves that there's a problem.***

In recent times, however, largely because of a provision of the 1984 Federal Child Support Enforcement Amendments, and of the Family Support Act of 1988 passed by Congress, by which all states were required to provide some type of formula or child-support guidelines by October 1989 on how much a parent should pay for child support, virtually every state in the nation now has a child support guideline schedule on the books which provides a set of numerical formulas for setting child-support awards. Under the circumstances, to set a child support amount, all that you would practically need to do is simply to follow the percentage guidelines or formula set forth in your given state's rules (unless, however, you can prove that the percentage amount would be unfair in your particular situation.)

In general, each state's guidelines require that the non-custodial parent (unless he lacks sufficient income to do so) must provide a specific level of monthly support to the parent having custody of the child. Furthermore, a common feature of today's child support arrangements is to provide for other non-monetary needs of the children that go beyond simply the monthly payment. For example, in addition to his paying support of a set amount of money, the supporting parent may also be required to carry health insurance on the children, or pay for their medical bills, or to provide life insurance for the custodial parent as the sole beneficiary.

As stated above, generally provided for under each state's divorcing procedures are specific statutory child support guidelines for meeting the state's child support obligation. *The good news for a do-it-yourselfer who is doing his or her own settlement agreement or divorce, is that in the present times virtually every state has a package of forms giving the approved guidelines and percentage standards for child support which are often readily available from the state's Family and Divorce Courts, as well as from the state's Department of Social Services*. Specific worksheets for use in working out the exact amounts of support to be paid are generally a part of the state's official guideline package of forms. If you are unable to find these forms otherwise, always ask the divorce clerk of your court for where you can obtain them or for copies of the local child support guidelines or rules that might be in effect.

To conclude this topic, perhaps a word of advice may be appropriate and useful as the ultimate 'guideline' to aid you in the making of your final determination as to what is the 'fair' amount of child support to ask from your spouse. One knowledgeable analyst probably says it as well as anyone, as follows:[11]

> "The [child support] guidelines provided [by the state laws] are just that: guidelines. They are not intended to be an ultimate method for determining support payments in all cases. They should be reviewed and used while considering all of the other relevant factors in your particular situation. The determination of the proper amount of child support in each case will always be difficult. ***A careful balance must be obtained between providing an adequate level of support and overburdening the parent who must pay the support. If the support payments are set at a level which becomes a tremendous financial burden to the paying parent, there will be a tendency and temptation to default on the payments. On the other hand, if the payments are too low, the child will suffer the consequences.***
>
> Both parents must work together carefully to actually determine a fair and reasonable amount of support. Care must be taken to keep the negotiations on a mature and rational basis. Discussions involving child support have the very real potential of deteriorating into hostile arguments. Of all of the aspects of divorce, child support obligations have spawned more post-divorce lawsuits than any other." [Emphasis added by the present writer]

---

[10] Siegel, op. cit. p. 126

[11] Starz, *Divorcing Yourself: The National No-Fault Divorce Kit* p. 122

H. OTHER ISSUES

Other issues that may arise in a settlement agreement or divorce situation, though not frequently with most couples in uncontested situations, may concern agreement on who should have the right to claim the children (or some particular ones) as his/her dependents when filing the annual income tax return; whether or not the children should be educated in a private school or a particular religious denomination, or up to a certain level of education at the expense of the supporting parent; whether one or the other parent should be responsible for the future medical bills and expenditures of the children (or spouse); and whether a parent is forbidden to take the child(ren) outside certain boundaries of the city or state without the written consent of the other parent, etc.

These matters do not occur as issues often. They rarely become problems with the overwhelming majority of divorcing couples. However, if you happen to think any of them might become a problem in your situation, there is a simple practical solution: just include a provision in your divorce papers (essentially in your "Petition" or "Complaint" and the "Final Judgment" papers, or even in your settlement agreement, if applicable) spelling out exactly such terms and conditions as you would want, or as have been agreed upon by the parties.

Statement Of Proposed Plan Of Equitable Settlement

Husband's Name: ______________________ **Wife's Name:**____________________________
Address: _____________________________ **Address:** ______________________________

STATEMENT OF MR/MRS ....;
(Name of Maker)

(a) The following assets are claimed to be joint marital property still undivided (if any):

(B) The following assets are claimed to be separate property owned by me:

(c) Following debts or liabilities are allocable to specific assets:

Debt or Liability Asset (state whether marital or separate)

(d) **THIS AMOUNT IS REQUESTED BY ME FOR MAINTENANCE** (if any): $.......... per ....(week, month, etc.) *Make this request for maintenance based on the following probable factors and consideration:*

1. Income of Husband
   At time of marriage ....
   At this time ....

2. Income of Wife
   At time of marriage ....
   At this time ....

3. Property of Husband
   At time of marriage:

   At this time:

4. Property of Wife
   At time of marriage:

   At this time:

5. Age of Husband .... Age of Wife ....

6. Duration of marriage (relationship): ....years ....months

7. Person having need (if any): .... Present and future capacity to be
   Husband/Wife
   self-supporting:

8. Time and training necessary for person having need to become self-supporting:

9. Number of children of the marriage of the marriage (relationship): ....
   Party (ies) with whom they reside: ....

10. Standard of living established during marriage (where practical and relevant):

11. Tax consequences to each party:

12. Contributions and services of party seeking maintenance to business, career or career potential of other party:

13. Wasteful dissipation of family assets by either spouse, any:

14. Any other factor (s) you may deem just and equitable:

(e) **MY PROPOSAL FOR EQUITABLE DISTRIBUTION OF PROPERTY** (based on the factors listed below), is:

I make the above proposed distribution based on the following factors and consideration:

(1) Income of Husband
   At time of marriage ....
   At this time ....

Income of Wife

At time of marriage ....

At this time ....

Property of Husband

At time of marriage:

At this time:

Property of Wife

At time of marriage:

At this time:

(2) Duration of marriage and health of parties:

Age of Husband .... Age of Wife ....

(3) Need of custodial parent to occupy or own marital residence and to use or own household effects:

(4) Loss of inheritance and pension rights:

(5) Maintenance award sought (see (d) above):

(6) Equitable claim to, interest in, or direct or indirect contribution made to acquisition of marital property by party not having title:

(7) Liquid or non-liquid character of marital property:

(8) Probable future financial circumstances of each party:

(9) Impossibility or difficulty of evaluating any component asset or interest in business, corporation or profession, and economic desirability of retaining such asset or interest intact and free from any claim or interference by other party:

(10) Any other factor (s):

(f) Proposal for a distributive award, including showing of need for a distributive award:

(g) **PROPOSED PLAN FOR CHILD SUPPORT** (if applicable), is as follows (based on the factors below):

(1) Financial resources of custodial and non-custodial parent [see d(1), above]
Financial resources of child(ren):

(2) Physical and emotional health of child(ren):

Educational and vocational needs and aptitudes of child(ren):

(3) Standard of living of child(ren) had marriage not dissolved:

(4) Non-monetary contributions of parents to child(ren):

(h) **MY PROPOSED PLAN FOR CUSTODY AND VISITATION** are as follows, including reasons:

Date: .... Signed: ....
(husband/wife)

CHAPTER 4

SEPARATION AND PROPERTY SETTLEMENT AGREEMENTS COMPARED: WHAT THEY ARE, WHAT THEY'RE USED FOR, AND THE BASIC LEGAL REQUIREMENTS FOR EACH TYPE

A. Living-Together Agreements in General

Under the laws of just about every state in the nation, parties who are about to be married may enter into an appropriate Premarital (also called pre-nuptial) Agreement. Likewise, parties who are unmarried may enter into an appropriate Cohabitation or Living-Together agreement. And parties, whether married or unmarried, may also enter into a valid Property Settlement Agreement before, during, or after marriage; and following the separation of the (married) parties, they may enter into a Separation Agreement. If a couple is married, at the moment the relationship comes into being, certain legal rights and duties spring into being. And, on the other side of the spectrum, if a couple is unmarried but living together, certain legal rights and duties they may otherwise think they have do not actually spring up. These rights and duties may, however, be varied by the signing of a valid Premarital Agreement for a couple that later went on to be married, or by the signing of a valid Cohabitation or Living-together Agreement, for a couple that never got married. In the absence of a Premarital Agreement (or a Cohabitation Agreement for the never-married couple), these rights and duties (or lack thereof, for the never married) continue, even when the parties separate, until such time as the parties enter into a valid separation or property agreement, or until their rights and duties are decided upon by a court of law.

In this chapter, we shall essentially focus on the legal significance of marriage (or non-marriage) as it relates to having a written agreement, the legal rights and consequences of separation, and how these rights and duties are affected by agreements entered into by the parties to the relationship.

B. The Nature of Separation

First, a definition of the term. What is (marital) *"separation"*? Basically, a marital separation is a separation between a husband and wife that is recognized and enforceable under the matrimonial laws of a state. Couples are, in effect, told it is sanctioned in the eyes of the law for them to separate and live apart from each other, while still technically remaining married. (It's sometimes called "partial divorce.") To put it another way, separation refers to a cessation of cohabitation (living together) by a husband and wife; it's a state of affairs that occurs when a husband and wife suspend marital relations but without a dissolution of the marriage relationship.

For our purposes in this manual, what is fundamental for you to take note of here, with respect to *marital separation*, is that in the absence of some sort of valid agreement between the parties, say a premarital agreement or separation and /or property settlement agreement, the rights and obligations which arose as a result of the marriage are not affected or terminated by the separation of a husband and wife. To be sure, there are some rights that may be lost or waived, depending upon the facts and the circumstances surrounding each case (e.g. the right to indulge in continued regular sexual relations). By and large, however, those rights and duties, or at least a good number of them — e.g., the right, with some qualifications*, to enforce cohabitation between married couples, the duty of the supporting spouse to support the dependent spouse or children, and certain rights under the inheritance and property laws — remain intact, or may at least be asserted. The rights do not terminate during the separation simply because the parties are living in a state of separation — until, that is, they are determined by a court of law, or are agreed upon by the parties in a written separation and/or property settlement agreement.

On the other hand, there are a number of legal rights and duties of the parties during the period of separation that may at best be somewhat confusing to parties until, again, they are settled either by a valid settlement agreement or by the determination of a court — e.g., the obligation of one spouse to provide for the support and maintenance of the other spouse, or the support, custody and visitation rights of parents with the minor children of the marriage, etc.

C. Why Would One Want To Get A Separation Arrangement?

As happens often, after a countless series of emotional bouts, often involving long and torturous agitations and deliberations, a couple may have come to that final realization that their marriage has "had it". It may dawn on both sides that their marriage is dead, and (as one lawyer put it), that "all that is left is to give it a decent burial". This couple may still be handicapped, nevertheless, and may not be able to go ahead with a divorce action right away. The problem may be: (1) inability to afford the legal costs of obtaining a divorce at the moment; or (2) that the couple lacks an acceptable legal "ground" for a divorce right now; or (3) that the couple simply lacks the emotional stamina to face an absolute divorce right now, and needs a less drastic arrangement for the time being to allow them a "cooling off" time to kind of "sort things out" more gradually.

Couples faced with a situation such as this, generally have one recourse: A LEGAL SEPARATION (by written agreement or court order).

One matrimonial lawyer with a long legal practice in the field, explains it this way:

> "There are two primary reasons to get a separation agreement. In some of those states that do not recognize no-fault law, New York for example, you can get a divorce solely on the basis of one year's separation; thus a separation agreement is a necessary prerequisite to a divorce action. The second reason to obtain such an agreement is that some people are genuinely uncertain as to whether or not they want a divorce. For these people a separation acts as a kind of trial divorce."**

D. Separation Agreement In Combination With Property Agreement

The distinction between a *"separation"* agreement and a *"property"* agreement could be unnecessarily technical, and may, in the end, at best be of interest only to the lawyers and the technicians of the law mesmerized by the fine details of law. But, under the laws of most states, basically for a valid *separation* agreement to obtain, a physical separation of the parties must have already occurred, or physical separation must actually follow immediately after the signing of the agreement. That is, a *separation is validly entered into only when the parties have already separated or intend to separate immediately following the signing of the agreement.* A property settlement agreement, on the other hand, can be validly entered into even without marriage, as when it's between an unmarried couple, or it can be entered into before marriage, as in the case of the premarital agreement, or during marriage, or following a separation of the (marital) parties. When the term property settlement agreement is spoken of within the context of family law practice, it's primarily concerned with the allocation of property between couples, whether married or otherwise, and, perhaps, other "ancillary" issues, such as child custody and visitation, alimony, and the

---

** Generally, upon physical separation in the absence of a written agreement or a court order to the contrary, either spouse may return to the marital home and resume cohabitation without excluding the other, providing he or she does not "criminally trespass" under the state's criminal trespass statute to do so. In brief, unless a spouse is forbidden by a court order to enter the marital premises, or the court, upon some determination that there is an "immediate and present danger" that acts of violence may be committed, has granted possession of the residence to one spouse to the exclusion of the other, a spouse has a right to return to the marital home and resume cohabitation or otherwise make efforts to effect reconciliation.

** Koff, *Love and The Law*, p. 174

like. And, as earlier stated, a settlement agreement could be legitimately entered into between married persons, as well as between non-married persons who are just cohabitating (or not even cohabitating) with each other, in a heterosexual or a homosexual relationship.

Fortunately, though, for the average reader's purposes the issue of having to make a distinction between a "separation" agreement and a "property" settlement agreement is greatly simplified by the fact that a separation agreement may be simply combined with a property settlement. Indeed, the *pure* separation agreement type is used in only limited cases, in a situation where the parties have no property rights at issue, such as in the case of the young married couple with no children and few, if any assets. In practice the more common approach among informed lawyers and others who draft such agreements, is to *combine* the separation agreement with the property agreement. However, in order to still preserve some sense of distinction between the two and thus avoid any potential pitfalls from intermingling the two, the better practice, experts contend, is simply to divide the agreement (which presumably contains elements of both separation and settlement of property rights) into distinct parts and sub-headings.*

E. The Main Practical Legal Purposes For Which Separation/Settlement Agreements Are Used

In the final analysis, as a practical matter, the distinction between a Separation and Property Settlement Agreement may be academic for the average person's purposes. For it may not matter which specific type of agreement you are talking about, or whether you are talking about a marital or nonmarital situation; ***the prime object and use for which couples' agreement of any sort is made, is essentially the same: namely, they are made in preparation for or in the process of a divorce (or breakup) action to dissolve a marriage or relationship.*** Such an agreement [which is often also called a "stipulation" or a "petition " in certain jurisdictions] become, then, the document by which couples (whether married or otherwise) set forth how they want to allocate their property and income upon divorce or a breakup, including other relevant issues, such as support, custody and visitation of their children, etc. ***In either case, by defining privately and BEFOREHAND the rights, obligations and entitlements of each party in the event of difficulties in the relationship, or doing so right after it has become clear to the parties that the relationship is headed for an eventual break-up, you minimize having to unnecessarily enrich the lawyers in what could otherwise be a bitter, protracted, costly battle in court.***

Thus, as a matter of practical reality, among most legal practitioners in the field of matrimonial law, separation or property settlement agreements are generally viewed today as, above everything else, a wise and least painful tool for "planning" or "negotiating" an eventual divorce. In the words of one Washington D.C. divorce lawyer, it is now "the practical device used by a husband and wife about to embark on the road to divorce; the basic instrument to effectuate a compatible divorce."

In years gone by, under the old system in operation during the pre-no fault days, the governing philosophy then operating was that any agreement or arrangement which appeared to have made it easier to dissolve a marriage or for couples to separate, was "against public policy." Such agreements or arrangements were therefore discouraged and frowned upon by the courts. Not so any more, though! ***Today, under the "new morality" of no-fault philosophy in settling marital affairs, the courts are more interested in one thing and one thing only: speeding up and smoothly resolving the process of dissolving the marriage and dividing up the common property among couples who wish to split.***

One legally acceptable tool by which this is frequently accomplished, is through the use of Written Agreements (or "stipulations") by couples. Today, most states now have laws or legal interpretations on the books by which the

---

* The courts, analysts contend, have made a distinction between the two [see, for example, Buffington, v. Buffington, 69 N.C. App. 138, 354. S.E. 2nd 291 (1987)]. Hence, the better practice is to divide an agreement into distinct parts. The distinction that can be made between separation agreements and property agreements, and the supposed consequences of not properly distinguishing between the two, can be summarized as follows: (1) a party's obligation under a property settlement may be discharged in bankruptcy, whereas alimony and child support are nondischargeable in Bankruptcy; (2) a party's alimony under a property settlement will survive death or remarriage and will be a claim against a deceased spouse's estate, whereas alimony normally terminates on the remarriage of the dependent spouse or the death of either party; (3) payments which are made in settlement of property rights are not modifiable without the consent of the parties; however, such payments may be construed as alimony and may become modifiable if the agreement be incorporated into a court judgment; and (4) a property settlement agreement is enforceable notwithstanding a resumption of marital relations, whereas the executory provisions of the separation agreement are unenforceable upon a resumption of marital relations [Lloyd T. Kelso, *North Carolina Divorce, Alimony and Child Custody, with Forms*, 2nd ed., (the Harrison Co., Norcross Ga 1989) p. 23, citing the statutory authorities and judicial decisions in support thereof].

provisions of a separation agreement, or other "stipulation" or written agreement, worked out by couples on just about anything (the state of their marriage, child custody or visitation rights or support, division of property, etc.) are accepted by the courts as the ***"grounds"*** or the primary basis for eventual settlement.*

The way it generally works out these days in most states is this: when a couple has a valid separation or other written settlement agreement (or separation decree), one or both of the spouses would be allowed to use that document either as a sufficient "ground" or basis for a divorce at a later date, or as the basis upon which the terms of a later court settlement is based. Thus, rather than leave the matters completely to chance or uncertainty or to an unpredictable judge at the very time of final settlement or divorce, the provisions of a separation and settlement agreement (or separation decree) previously drawn up and signed by the parties are, in effect, simply incorporated into the divorce decree, with little or no modifications. Because of this reality, *many divorce lawyers now view a separation agreement as a "real passport" to a divorce, a "negotiated" and "compatible" method of achieving a divorce*; and state legislators and judges who preside over divorce and matrimonial issues now favor, even love,** situations where the partners themselves have already worked out and signed a settlement agreement before coming to trial.

The following provisions of different states laws are typical of the prevailing philosophy among the ever-growing list of no-fault divorce states in the country, providing a few examples of how important having a good written settlement or separation agreement is often viewed in today's divorce courtrooms:

The ***Connecticut divorce statute*** (Conn. General Statute, Sec. 46-47), provides:

> "When the parties (i.e., the spouses) submit a written stipulation that their marriage has broken down irretrievably, or when both parties are physically present in court and have submitted an agreement concerning the custody, care, education, visitation, maintenance and support of their children, the testimony of either party in support of that conclusion shall be sufficient and the court shall make a finding that such marriage break down has (in fact) occurred..."

The ***Colorado Divorce statute*** (Revised Statutes, Sec. 14-10-110) provides:

> "If both of the parties, by petition or otherwise, have stated under oath or affirmation that the marriage is irretrievably broken, or one of the parties has so stated and the other has not denied it, there is a presumption of such fact, and unless controverted by evidence, the court shall, after a hearing, make a finding that the marriage is irretrievably broken."

The ***Pennsylvania no-fault divorce statute*** [Penn. Divorce Code, Sec 3301 (d)] provides, for another example:

> "The court may grant a divorce where a [written]complaint has been filed alleging that the marriage is irrevocably broken and an affidavit has been filed alleging that the parties have lived separate and apart for a period of at least two years, and that the marriage is irrevocably broken, and the defendant either: (i) Does not deny the allegation set forth in the affidavit; or (ii) Denies one or more of the allegations set forth in the affidavit, but after notice and hearing, the court determines that the parties have lived separate and apart for a period of at least two years and that the marriage is irretrievably broken..."

---

* The Uniform Marriage and Divorce Act of 1970, from which the laws of most no-fault divorce states borrowed their moral impetus, provides as follows: "To promote amicable settlement of disputes between parties to a marriage...(they) may enter into a written separation agreement...(and) in a proceeding for dissolution of marriage or for legal separation, the terms of the separation agreement...are binding upon the court unless it finds...the agreement unconscionable." The drafters of this act then acknowledged in a special "Note", that "this section, entirely reverses the older view that property settlement agreements are against public policy because They tend to promote divorce." (See also Appendix A for the "grounds" for securing a divorce in all 50 states.)

** One Illinois judge expressed the courts' preference this way: "Parties to divorce suits are to be commended for their attempt to settle their property differences amicably. This not only saves the courts from being fraught with details and the necessity of repeated, recurrent hearings, but leads to better feelings and peace of mind..." Quoted from "Everything You've Always Wanted to Know About the Law" by Edward E. Colby, p. 255.

The *Mississippi statute* based on the no fault ground of "irreconcilable differences" [Miss. Code Ann. ζ93-5-2], provides:

> "No divorce shall be granted on the ground of irreconcilable differences unless the court shall find in its decree that the parties have made adequate and sufficient provisions by written agreement for the custody and maintenance of any children of that marriage and for the settlement of any property rights between the parties..."

The *Tennessee Statute* based on the no-fault ground of "irreconcilable differences" [Tenn. Code ζ36-4-103], provided:

> No divorce shall be granted on the ground of irreconcilable differences unless the court shall affirmably find in its decree that the parties have made adequate and sufficient provisions by written agreement for the custody and maintenance of any children of that marriage and for the equitable settlement of any property rights between the parties..."

Indeed, to sum it all up, from an examination of all the statutory variations, it seems quite clear that a major underlying rationale behind both the living apart ground, in particular, and the no-fault category of grounds, in general, is that the legislatures and the courts simply view the very act of separation and living apart as an objective expression of a marriage that is broken. Thus, first, in those states which use the no-fault type of grounds such as 'irretrievable breakdown of the marriage relationship' and 'incompatibility', the mere act of separation and living apart is often designated as a manifestation or proof of such a legal ground. Then, there is another group of states where separation and living apart is specifically designated under the law as a legal ground for getting a divorce.

States Having Living Separate and Apart As A Specific Ground For Divorce

The following are the states which specifically have the act of living separate and apart as the ground for getting a divorce (by a written agreement or otherwise):

1. Arkansas (3 years)
2. Connecticut (18 months due to incompatibility
3. District of Columbia
   (6 months voluntary; 1 year involuntary)
4. Hawaii (2 years)
5. Idaho (5 years)
6. Louisiana (2 Years)
7. Maryland (1 year voluntary; 3 years involuntary)
8. Nevada (1 year in court's discretion)
9. New Hampshire
10. New Jersey (18 months)
11. North Carolina (1 year)
12. Ohio (2 years)
13. Puerto Rico (2 years)
14. Rhode Island (3 years)
15. South Carolina (3 years)
16. Texas (3 years)
17. Vermont (6 months)
18. Virginia (1 year)
19. West Virginia (2 years)

States Allowing For Conversion From Judicial Separation To Divorce

In the following states, a decree of judicial separation or separate maintenance can be converted into a decree of absolute divorce after a certain period of time:

1. Alabama (2 years after decree of judicial separation)
2. Connecticut (any time after separation decree)
3. District of Columbia (after legal separation has continued for 6 months voluntarily or for 1 year)
4. Hawaii (2 years separation)
5. Louisiana (1 year from signing decree of separation)
6. New York (1 year living apart pursuant to decree of separation)

7. North Dakota (4 years living apart after decree of separation)
8. Tennessee (2 years after decree of separation)
9. Utah (3 years living apart under decree of separate maintenance of any state)
10. Wisconsin (not earlier than 1 year after entry of decree of legal separation or by stipulation of both parties)

F. The Two Basic Kinds Of Legal Separation

There are two basic types of legal separation:

Type 1 - Separation By Court Order (or Decree)

Also known as "Separation Judgment", "Separation Order", this is separation and living apart based on a court order. The elements of this form of legal separation are rather simple: Firstly, the court shall have rendered a judgment (court order) of separation, ordering separation by the couple; secondly, in compliance with that order, the couple shall have lived *continuously* apart without interruption or reconciliation for that length of time (or more) stipulated under the given state's law for filing for divorce using separation-by-court-order (or plain separation) as the ground.

Type 2 - Separation By Written Agreement

This is a separation and living apart based on a written agreement worked out and signed between a husband and wife. The requirements for qualifying under this ground are almost the same as with court-ordered separation situation above. The only difference is rather obvious: here, the separation and living apart by the parties shall have been occasioned by a formal ***written agreement*** agreed to and signed by the couple, rather than by court order. And, as in the case of separation by court order, the parties would have thereafter actually lived separate and apart from each other for a continuous period of time stipulated under the law, and shall not have reconciled or lived together as man and wife during that time.

G. Which Of The Two Kinds Of Legal Separation Should One Use?

For a variety of reasons, most practitioners prefer the Type 2 separation.* Some of the reasons for this are the following:

1. Normally, one can accomplish in an agreement everything the court can establish by a decree, and even more. Yet, as a rule, separation by a decree is generally the far more expensive of the two methods — costing anywhere from an average of $600 to $1,500 per couple for the simplest variety in a state like New York, and involving the whole panoply of traditional court procedures: judges and lawyers, court clerks, legal (the lawyers') fees, filing requirements and filing fees, courtroom trials and hearings, etc.

2. Separation by court decree is generally a far more drawn-out and more "public" affair than its counterpart—involving all the "washing of dirty linen in the public" dimension that most people would rather avoid.

For example, in order to get a separation by court decree, you would first have to bring a suit in court against your spouse; then you must allege and prove specific legal "grounds" against him or her as prescribed by law. On the other hand, separation by a written agreement is made without having to go to any court, or to establish any grounds.

---

* The one supposed "advantage" which the court-decreed type of legal separation is said to have over separation by written agreement, is that the court-decreed separation supposedly affords one spouse the special remedy of hauling the other one into court, if he should violate or fail to live up to the terms of the decree, and having him charged with "contempt of court" (i.e., not obeying a court order). On the other hand, it is argued, in a case involving the violation of the terms of a written agreement, all that the other spouse can do is to sue the violator to court to demand that the terms of the agreement to enforced.

The argument, then, is that it is a far more serious matter to be "in contempt of the court" than to be "in contempt of the other spouse." Maybe. Just maybe. For, as a practical matter, the real advantage of a separation by court decree over separation by written agreement is actually very minimal, if any. First of all, we have long gone past the era when a husband (or wife, for that matter) gets sent to jail for non-support or alimony; if a husband really doesn't voluntarily want to comply with a court's child support or alimony orders, there's not quite much the courts can do about it in any case. Sending him to jail would not change that, and the courts rarely try that nowadays. If the worse comes to the worst, some have been known to skip town, run to a far away (or even foreign) state and conceal their whereabouts. In practice, then, the two types of legal separation do not afford dramatically different remedies after all.

3. Another reason why separation by agreement is generally preferred, is because specific arrangements for support, custody, and/or the education of the children, etc., can be tailored exactly to suit special individual circumstances. In

a court decree situation, on the other hand, the judge being a total stranger, after all, is in no better position than the couples themselves to know what serves the best interests of a couple, what the spouses or their children need or like the most, etc.

4. Another important reason is this: legal actions brought by one or both spouses to secure a court-ordered separation, ultimately ends up being what people in legal circles call "a road to nowhere," in any event. In other words, while the procedure and expenditures involved in obtaining a court-ordered separation decree are almost the same as the ones involved in obtaining an actual final divorce, nevertheless a court-ordered separation decree does not confer a divorce or dissolution of the marriage. All it does for a couple is simply allow them to live apart "legally". But they still remain married for a practical legal purposes — the same as a separation by written agreement would do for the couple. But the separation agreement is far less involved or expensive than court-ordered separation! If, in the future, the couple with a court-ordered separation seeks to be completely divorced from each other, they must now bring another (i.e. a second) suit for that, and go over the same trouble and court expense all over again.

In a word, separation "by decree" generally involves going through the same court procedures and emotional and financial expenditures, twice. Separation "by a written agreement" does not. So, why travel through the expensive "road to nowhere", the road of a court-ordered separation decree? When you can travel through that same road *inexpensively* — by using a written agreement?

H. Can You Properly Draw Up Your Own Separation Agreement Without A Lawyer?

The answer is YES, YES, YES. You not only can, you indeed should! First of all, one fundamental point needs to be gotten perfectly into the minds and heads of everyone right away. That point is this: ***the correctness or the legal validity of a separation or settlement agreement or, for that matter, any legal contract or agreement of whatever kind, does not, in any way, depend on what the professional calling or title of its preparer is. Not at all!*** Generally speaking, any agreement voluntarily drawn up, signed and agreed to by any two (or more) adults themselves, may be just as legally valid as the one drawn up by the world's best lawyer, and the courts will normally give full recognition to such an agreement — as long as it meets certain basic tests of reasonableness, mutual fairness, clarity and public policy propriety. It is completely irrelevant whether such an agreement was drawn up by a lawyer, a doctor, a mailman, or what have you!

The second point is: It's the commonly acknowledged **legal** and civil ***right*** of every American, who so prefers, to draw up his or her own legal papers, and even represent himself in any legal proceedings involving civil matters. That's what the courts have consistently ruled — whether it be in a divorce, bankruptcy, probate, tenant-landlord disputes, will-drafting, incorporating your business, or what have you. That's the law! The only relevant question you really ought to concern yourself with is this: DO I KNOW HOW TO PROPERLY DRAW UP AN AGREEMENT THAT MEETS THE MINIMUM LEGAL STANDARDS? Well, if you can say "yes" to this basic question (and what else is this manual for!), then you really don't have to hire a lawyer to do the agreement for you — unless, of course, you're rich, or enjoy throwing moneys away, or just plain lazy!

The Third point: Finally, there's an even more important issue here for you from your standpoint as a consumer. ***And that is that, you not only can do it yourself, you should.*** There are just so many advantages and benefits for you in doing it yourself that it will be highly perplexing if you were to do otherwise: it's much cheaper doing it yourself; you can better keep matters simple and agreeable without a lawyer's involvement; you get to make the major decisions on your own life doing it yourself, and so on and on, as fully elaborated in Chapter 2 (see, esp. pp. 6 -10). So, why wouldn't you rather just do the agreement yourselves (you and your spouse), and leave the lawyer out of it!

I. The Basic Prerequisites For A Good Couples' Agreement Of Any Kind

If you and your spouse (or non-marital partner) can meet the following conditions in a self-made agreement, you can be almost certain that your written agreement (of any kind) would be just as good as any drawn up by the best lawyer in the business:

1. Does there exist, between you and your spouse, a mutual and free consent or understanding to separate or to do what you propose? ***This is an absolute Number One requirement for a good settlement agreement,*** because, if you do have this, everything else frequently works out pretty well. To have a valid agreement, each of you shall have signed the agreement without force or coercion, and absolutely by the free will of each individual.

2. Each spouse should read the contents of the agreement (or have them read to him or her), and each shall have had a fairly good understanding of the terms and provisions of the agreement to which he or she puts his/her signature at the time.

3. There shall have been an absolute exercise of honesty and good faith on both sides; that is, a full disclosure of all relevant facts, and no fraud or material misrepresentation of assets or circumstances by either the husband or wife.

4. The agreement itself should appear generally fair, free of fraud, and even-handed to both sides, and more especially, to the general welfare and security of the minor child(ren), if there are any.

5. The spouses entering into the agreement must both be "competent" to do so — that is, each must be sane, not underage, and generally in full control of his or her mind ***at the time*** of the negotiations and signing of the agreement.

6. Each side should make certain that he or she provides something of value — "consideration" in legal jargon — to the other side. That is, each person who promises to do or give something in the relationship, should also get something in return, though not necessarily something identical or nominally equal in value. (A "consideration" might be something as simple as a promise to share the living-together expenses, say 50-50; or a promise by one party to pay off a common debt in return for a promise by the other party not to sue in the future over past acts or obligations; or one partner might promise to give up his or her job to care for the household, in return for the promise by the other to pay the household expenses for a certain period of time.)

7. No provision promoting divorce or providing to *specifically* secure a divorce, or to commit a crime or otherwise engage in anything illegal or against "public policy,"* shall have been included in the agreement. In brief, a provision is deemed to be against policy if it attempts by its provisions to change the normal duties and responsibilities which arise by virtue of the marital status.

8. To best maintain its validity, your separation agreement shall have *already* taken place, or else it should be contemplated and be immediately followed by, actual separation upon the signing of the agreement. (An agreement for a future separation is invalid as it is regarded as promotion of divorce, and hence contrary to public policy. You should note, though, that not all jurisdictions in the nation require that the parties be actually physically living in different residences in order to meet its definition of being separated.)

---

*See pp. 37-8 for more on what constitutes "public policy."

See, for example, Kentucky, KRS 703.170 (1), which states in part "No decree shall be entered until the parties have lived apart for sixty (60) days. Living apart shall include living under the same roof without sexual cohabitation." And Delaware defines "separation" under its rules [Delaware Code Annotated ζ1503 (7)] as "living separate and apart for six or more months immediately preceding the ruling [on a divorce petition]... except that no period of separation is required with respect to marriage characterized under [ζ1505 (b) (2) of this title [which refers to 'separation caused by respondent's misconduct' as a ground for divorce]; and separation may commence and/or continue while both parties reside under the same roof, provided during such period the parties occupy several bedrooms and do not have sexual relations with each other."

CHAPTER 5

SOME DON'TS: THE LIMITATIONS OF A LEGAL SEPARATION

Are there certain things a separation agreement (or legal separation of any kind) may not provide for? The answer is a resounding yes.

Basically, what is most important to remember is that a separation (or settlement) agreement does not, at all, mean—and is not the same thing as — a divorce or termination of the marriage. A separation agreement (or court decree) means just what it says: it's just an agreement that entitles you to legally separate and live apart from each other, often with some allocations of marital property, children, support, and so on, to one party or the other, *but nothing more*. For all intents and purposes, the spouses remain married in the eyes of the law. This means, in other words, that (at least in theory), each spouse would still retain many of the same rights, obligations and prohibitions commonly expected of married couples.

HERE ARE SOME OF THOSE RIGHTS, OBLIGATIONS AND PROHIBITIONS:

1. Neither the wife nor the husband may engage in sexual relations with other persons (it's still adultery if they do); indeed, both parties are, in theory at least (and often in theory only), expected to continue to have sexual relations with each other, only.

2. A Separation Agreement (or decree) does not relieve a husband (or wife) from his liability to support his wife, especially if she's needful,* and even when an agreement provides that a wife voluntarily waives (i.e., gives up) her right to claim support, the courts would not generally honor or enforce that provision, particularly if and when she's needful. Indeed, this is one reason a separation agreement is today often made a part and parcel of settlement agreement, as it is essentially futile in the eye of the law to have separation without the settlement of the collateral marital issues involved in the relationship.

(The New York state's courts, for example, have ruled that a separation agreement in which the wife agrees not to demand any sums for alimony or support violates the state's General Obligations Law, which prohibits contracts relieving the husband from his liability to support his wife; and that even when a husband, in complying with the terms of a separation agreement, makes a lump-sum payment to the wife "in full fulfillment" of his obligations to her, this would also be a violation of the General Obligations Law. According to this decision, support is a continuing obligation that cannot be terminated by making just one lump-sum payment, but must be measured periodically.)

* Even in this "age of women's equality" in the nation, the common practice in most states, either by law or by precedent, is not to grant the support of a husband by a wife, even if the husband's financial needs and the wife's ability to pay would warrant that. However, perhaps a recent U.S. Supreme Court decision outlawing state laws which specifically provide for alimony to the wife only, may — just may — change that in practical terms although that still remains to be seen. Note that certain courts have held, however, that where a wife, who is otherwise able, clearly refuses to seek an independent means of income, or voluntarily leaves a well-paying job to seek, say, a college degree or to travel, the husband may not be compelled to support her any further.

3. A Separation agreement does not relieve or exempt either parent of a minor child, and especially the father, from liability to support the child, and if an agreement should provide something contrary, it would rarely be accepted or enforced by the courts. Most courts view the obligation of the parents to support their children as "a basic and fundamental right belonging to the children which cannot be abrogated or derogated" by any separation or other agreements made between the parents. Furthermore, since marital agreements are usually not signed by the children themselves, anyway, the children are not necessarily bound by the terms of such agreements in any event.

4. A separation agreement may not generally disinherit a husband or wife from the property rights of the other spouse — **unless** the spouse involved had already been assigned a reasonable consideration (a thing of value) as the trade-off for her giving up the rights in the property retained by the other spouse.

5. In at least one state, the state of New York, the courts have ruled that where a separation agreement does not *specifically* provide that a "substantial change in financial circumstances"* of the husband may entitle him to a modification of an alimony or child support obligation, the husband is not relieved of such obligation to the extent provided for in the agreement.**

6. A separation agreement may not be "collusory"— that is, it may not (expressly) provide that the parties agree that the marriage should be dissolved, then or later.

NOTE: *Here's the interesting thing you have to take good note of, though:* *while the agreement may not* ***specifically*** *provide for this, it may, however, provide that if either or both spouses ever wish to file for a divorce at any time in the future, the separation agreement may be used as the basis, and the terms incorporated or "merged" into the resulting divorce decree, "in part" or "in whole." In other words, it's just a matter of making sure that at no place in the agreement did you explicitly say, in effect, "we want this marriage terminated!"*

7. A separation agreement (which, presumably, is otherwise fair and equitable) may provide that the wife (or husband, as the case may be) promises not to sue for increases in the amount of alimony or child support provided for in the agreement. However, when an agreement does not expressly make such a provision, the wife is not relieved of the right to ask for increments, especially when she can show that the terms of the agreement were not fair or equitable, in the first place.

8. Generally speaking, a separation agreement may not be clearly fair to one spouse, and clearly unfair to the other spouse, or to the children especially, where applicable. It may not provide for the parties to engage in unlawful activities, or in any act that is against "public policy"(e.g., prostitution, spouse-swapping, bigamy, remarriage while still married to the present spouse, sexual relations with a third party, non-support of the couple's children, and the like).

---

* Events such as these would be examples of a substantial change in financial circumstances: retirement or loss of a job, a cut in pay, disability, a major illness, a large inheritance or an increase in responsibility.

** The general rule, however, is that in cases of serious changes in the circumstance of the husband, the amounts set for child support or alimony payments may be modified, and a separation agreement which so provides is generally not invalid. Furthermore, a separation agreement may also provide that in case of any disagreement on whether a change in condition has, in fact, occurred, or on the amount by which child support or alimony is to be reduced or increased, the dispute may be submitted to a designated person or institution for settlement by a binding arbitration, and that the cost of litigating the agreement in court shall be borne by the party who is found to be at fault.

CHAPTER 6

LET'S NEGOTIATE AND DRAFT THE SEPARATION/SETTLEMENT AGREEMENT BETWEEN YOU AND YOUR SPOUSE: The Step-By-Step Procedures

A. Some Helpful Practical Procedures For Negotiating And Working Out A Good Agreement

Follow these procedures and formalities in negotiating and working out the terms of your agreement:

1. Each spouse should first hold preliminary "rap session" type discussions with a trusted confidant(s) or advisor(s) (they could be one's parents or relatives or trusted friends) about what the couple is contemplating doing. Run down, in general terms, the whole range of the issues, terms and provisions that persons in your particular circumstances might consider incorporating into an agreement. [Refer to chapter 3 as your primary guide]

2. Realize that in today's divorce or marital settlement climate when marriage is often viewed simply as an economic partnership, the central issue is essentially the "practical" and "economic" aspects of marriage and breakup — that is, MONEY, in a word!* What this means is that, assuming that there are some marital property actually accumulated and needing to be distributed in your situation — which is actually not quite the case in the vast majority of marriages — the very FIRST thing you'll need to do is to identify all the marital assets there are, and appraise their value. If you are among the vast majority of divorce seekers who own little or no property, in the first place, or among those falling under the so-called middle-class brackets who own not much more beyond, say, a modest home and perhaps a small corner grocery store or a similar small business, you may not have to do much investigating to determine how much marital property there is in the marriage, if any. Simply have both parties (you and your spouse or partner) complete, in full, a Statement of Account [see the Statement of Net Worth reproduced on page 88 for a sample]. Have each party swear to (notarize) each net worth statement and then exchange them. This way, when the actual pre-settlement negotiations start you will each have fully studied the statements and made relevant notes on them, and would have something to compare notes on and negotiate about at the negotiation sessions.

3. This point cannot be emphasized enough: **MOST IMPORTANTLY, BE THOROUGHLY PREPARED BEFOREHAND.** As one veteran marital settlement negotiator, a lawyer, put it, "A well-prepared client makes for a

---

* One observer, an experienced New York divorce lawyer, put it bluntly this way: "The rules of divorce [have] changed... and the emphasis has shifted from sin to economics. In today's climate, with marriage viewed as an economic partnership .... [consequently, being] familiar with the practical aspects of divorce is necessary...Instead of hiring detectives to raid motel rooms in search of adulterous behavior, today's attorneys [or divorce filers] must often be prepared to trade monetary transactions, locate and determine the value of certain assets, and work closely with accountants and appraisers" Koff, in "*Love and The Law,*" p. 166

well prepared attorney, which helps to achieve the best possible result." You should be certain to come to the negotiations fully armed with certain essential information on the "facts" as well as the "law" on your rights, entitlements and obligations [Refer principally to Chapter 3 at pp. 13-28].

Here are, in brief, the kinds of essential information you should seek to assemble (and bring with you to the negotiations) on yourself, as well as on your spouse:

- A copy of any pre-existing prenuptial or marital agreements between the parties, if any.
- A detailed inventory of all property in your home, (including antiques, furniture, works of art, jewelry, and even appliances).
- A listing of your marital property, including real estate, automobiles, furniture, appliances, artwork, collections, computers, electronic equipment.
- A complete list, with account numbers, of joint bank accounts, certificates of deposit, stocks and bonds, retirement accounts, money-market funds, etc.
- A listing of your separate property, including jewelry, bank accounts, investments, real estate, etc.
- As complete a listing as possible of your spouse's separate property
- A list of all joint and separate debts, including mortgages, credit-card balances, car loans, etc.
- Copies of your joint tax returns for the past two or three years; and of your business or your spouse's jointly-operated business.
- A list of health, life, disability, homeowners, automobile, and other insurance policies
- Copies of all pertinent financial records: tax returns, recent pay stubs for you and your spouse, bank account statements, insurance documents, deeds, statements and records regarding items such as fringe benefits, pensions, personal expenses paid for by a business, tax-exempt investment income, etc.
- A diary of any facts pertinent to the family finances — e.g., any purchases of significant items made by the spouses, business meetings; any entertaining any of you did of a business nature, and, in fault states, any proof of adultery, cruel and inhuman treatment, abandonment, and so forth. Dated entries and names of any witnesses to events might be important.

Be aware that often many, perhaps most, of the items mentioned above (or contained in the various sample agreements used in the guidebook) may not be specifically relevant or applicable to your particular case. In general, however, much of the relevant information of financial nature that may be needed for effective negotiations on an average case is summed up in the STATEMENT OF NETWORTH on page 87, as well as in the STATEMENT OF PROPOSED PLAN OF EQUITABLE SETTLEMENT (p. 25), just in case you should need it.

Sometimes some of the information called for in the Networth statement may be missing from the statement your spouse gives you, or what is listed may be (or may seem to be) appreciably less than the actual value you expect. In truth, spouses have been known to attempt to hide assets (by, say, opening bank accounts unknown to their spouse or by purchasing property concealed to the spouse or by simply transferring title to another person. Or, some spouses may wastefully run up credit cards or empty out savings accounts by furiously spending them down just when a divorce seems to be looming. If you were to strongly suspect or know this for sure, it's perfectly within your rights to demand a good explanation of what happened and to insist that your spouse provide a more accurate accounting of the assets supposedly used up or hidden away so that such items can be accurately reported so that they may be included in any settlement. (If and when deemed necessary, an accountant could be hired to help you out, and to review all of your spouse's personal and/or business records as well as his (her) personal savings and checking accounts).

4. Get into discussions and negotiations with your spouse on the various issues of relevance in your case. [See chapter 3 for an idea about the typical issues, and the PROPOSED PLAN OF EQUITABLE SETTLEMENT form on p. 25, for an idea about the outlines of a possible settlement plan.] In such negotiations, seek to have both spouses vent out your stands fully, and participate freely in hammering out the terms that need to be provided in the agreement. The negotiations with your spouse (or partner) do not have to be face to face between the two of you. Quite to the contrary, because marriage breakup is often an emotionally charged matter, it may frequently be a good idea to do the negotiations from a distance — by phone, letters, exchange of draft agreements. On those rarer instances when the breakup is less contentious and more friendly, and the parties' emotions are under control, couples can of course get together and do the negotiating face-to-face.

5. If the separation is an amicable one, or at least a reasonably controlled one, then in that event that would be a situation where you and your spouse may each write a first draft of the agreement before getting together. [Use the form on p. 25, Proposed Plan Of Equitable Settlement, as an aid and sample in helping you draft the terms]• You will generally be summing up the general areas of agreement; and in the areas of disagreement you can put down what you want on the various issues, or the alternatives, what your objectives are; and then work from there. Then when the actual negotiations start, you may simply run through the various issues and together discuss the alternatives and make genuine, good faith efforts, to try to come to some compromises over matters that still remain unresolved.

On the other hand, where there are particularly major or sticky issues that cannot be resolved by the parties, this process won't work, and the parties may have to get together to negotiate more directly. Or, if all else fails, they may even have to resort to retaining an outside negotiator — a professional settlement "***mediator***" or an attorney who is trained specifically to help couples negotiate a reasonable settlement. (See p. 11 for the subject of negotiations through a mediator or a counseling service).

In fact, as fully explained in Chapter 2 of the manual (see, p. 11), these days an increasing number of couples who want to achieve their separation or divorce without much inter-personal fight or acrimony are turning to the use of impartial professional mediators to reach a settlement. For a national mediation organization which provides referrals to mediators meeting its strict requirements, contact:

The Academy of Family Mediators
P.O. Box 10501
Eugene, Or 97440
Telephone: (503) 345-1205

Note: *Whatever you do, though, try your darnest (both of you) to avoid ever having to bring in the lawyers in these negotiations! It could be the most deadly thing you ever did <u>against</u> yourselves!! [Refer, especially to chapter 2, sections E & G thereof, at pp. 6-8]*

6. To the extent necessary and practicable, be sure to give a general idea (emphasize!) in the agreement the extent of each party's intelligence, literacy, experience and general familiarity with or ability to understand the document he/she signed — though like the age of each party at the time of the agreement his and her level of education, previous marital experience, if any, how long each party has been widowed or divorced, if applicable, the degree of familiarity or previous experience with legal documents (or with attorneys), the extent, if any, to which a party (or both) has been a business person and dealt with the business world and valuation of property and investment, and the like.

B. Negotiating With Your Spouse Or Partner: Here's How The Actual Negotiating "Haggling" Process Works.

Just for an idea of the typical process, here's the negotiating atmosphere and scenario, as given by one expert with wide experience in countless marital settlement negotiations in an adult lifetime of practice as a divorce lawyer:

> "Once the marital property has been identified and its value ascertained, the next step is to divide it. Emotionally this is not always an easy task. People become attached to such possessions as a favorite chair, an antique, even a record collection. And there are especially strong emotional ties to family homes, places where one's children have grown up. You can divide property, but it's extremely difficult to divide memories, and that is often what happens in a divorce.

But the fact is that it must be done and there are two basic rules of property division in this country: community property [the states falling under this category require all property and earnings required AFTER the marriage to be shared equally between the spouses], and equitable distribution [meaning states requiring that all marital property be distributed 'equitably,' but not necessarily equally...]

Amicable negotiation is certainly the preferred method although in some divorces this is not always feasible. In fact, it's an old legal saw that in a fair settlement neither party is happy. But if both spouses are willing to negotiate a fair property settlement, the benefits are obvious. For one thing, they will avoid having a judge make an arbitrary decision, one that might not satisfy the needs or desires of either party.

With all the marital property on the table, negotiation can begin. It might be a simple matter of dividing assets by their declared value (which should be agreed to prior to the negotiation). There are several other elementary methods that might be employed. You might take turns choosing property from the pot, for instance. Or you might try the method parents sometimes use to avoid arguments among their children: 'You cut the cake, and your brother can choose the slice he wants.'

If negotiation doesn't work, you might want to consider trying mediation, a method that seems to be gaining in popularity.... [involving use of] the assistance of a professional mediator, often a social worker or attorney trained specifically to help couples negotiate a satisfactory settlement... [and] to facilitate agreement by offering objective, third-party alternatives... Successful mediation can save both time and money in divorce cases [and often includes the cost of preparing and filing the necessary settlement agreements and court papers...]

If neither negotiation nor mediation works, the last resort is to bring the action to trial where a judge will take the matter out of your hands and make the decision as to how the property is to be divided."

C. The Actual Drafting Of The Agreement

Once a general agreement or understanding is arrived at between you and your spouse, (whether it is by phone or mail or direct negotiation, or through a mediator or even a lawyer), the way is cleared for you to commence with the actual drafting of the Separation/Settlement Agreement. THIS IS WHERE THIS DO-IT-YOURSELF MANUAL KIT COMES IN HANDY. USING THE STEP-BY-STEP INSTRUCTIONS PROVIDED BELOW IN THIS SECTION AS YOUR AID AND GUIDE, YOU WILL THEN DRAW UP AN AGREEMENT GENERALLY AGREEABLE TO BOTH OF YOU — ***i.e., you simply write what and what you both agreed to into an agreement.*** As you go through the process of drawing up your separation/settlement agreement, bear in mind the major incidental issues that generally need to be worked out and resolved by such an agreement — property division, division of marital debts and bills, alimony, custody of children, child visitation rights, child support, etc., as applicable. [Indeed, refer directly to Chapter 3, at pp. 13-28 and follow closely therein the elaborate listing of the various typical issues, and the general legal principles (generally "community property" or "equitable distribution" rules) which govern their respective determinations]

Now, we come to the actual mechanical drafting of the written agreement. To begin the process, in the pages ahead (pp. 44-58), you'll find two different samples of a separation/settlement agreement, each involving a particular situation or circumstance:

Sample I: For a married couple with minor children, substantial marital property, and same pension rights. [see p. 44]

Sample 2: For a married couple with NO minor children, and with little or no property, and no pension rights [see p. 58]

Now, select either Sample #1 or 2, representing the sample form that is appropriate for your situation, and complete it by filling in the necessary information or optional range of information in the blank spaces in each paragraph. For any articles, paragraphs (or contents, or provisions) which may not be applicable in your case, simply cross that out and mark it so that it will not be included in your final drafted copy. (Note that for situations involving other types of couples, such as non-marital living together situations, the couple may use and adapt these same forms, but with the appropriate modifications made to reflect the non-marital status of the relationship.)

YOU MUST GO STEP-BY-STEP, STRICTLY IN ORDER

THIS IS VERY IMPORTANT: in preparing the draft agreement form, take it one (and only ONE) step at a time, following the items **EXACTLY** in the same numerical order in which they are listed in the manual. In each clause or paragraph you come to, first read it to understand what is called for. Then, go one step (and only one step) at a time according to the order of the numbering. ***Do not skip around from step to step or from page to page.***

Make Photocopies & Use them As Your "Practice" Worksheets

A good practice in preparing the drafts, is to make some photocopies of the sample form and use that photocopy as a "practice" worksheet. Fill in the appropriate information in all the photocopy Practice Sheets, from the first page to the last, and as you go along, if there are any paragraphs or provisions which do not apply to your particular situation, cross them out. You'll simply "pencil in" on the sample practice form, in the blank spaces, the appropriate words and statements for a given entry. In each instance, be sure that the words or statements you fill in or enter do clearly state exactly what you want to convey to yourselves and to everybody who reads them. CLUE: Ask yourself this question:

"Would a stranger reading these words or statements readily know what I'm trying to say? Would they make simple sense to him or her? Are my intentions clear, straightforward and unambiguous?" Then, after checking to make sure you have everything pretty much in order, type out the form, with all information fully filled in, on a final true sheet.

What To Do When You've Completed Making Up The Draft Copy Of Your Agreement

Let's assume you've finished writing up the initial practice drafts. There are a few little things left before you are done: TYPING OUT A FINAL PERFECT COPY OF THE AGREEMENT. Here's what you do. Now, run through the initial draft copy of your agreement, from its first page down; and, carefully and in order, type (or print) out on clear separate sheets of paper, the complete Agreement with the contents of each and every clause or paragraph that you filled in or checked off now included. Type (or print) out everything onto separate sheets of white paper to make out a final, true copy of your agreement. (Number the pages of your completed agreement at the top of each paper and be sure to provide at the bottom left corner of each paper, a space for you to initial and date the agreement.) You should make three (and only three) final copies of the Agreement; you may use carbon paper, but make sure that each copy is exactly the same in contents.)

Avoid erasing, crossing out or other corrections in your final draft to avoid any suspicions that might arise later that such changes might have been slipped in by someone other than you. (Note: if your final agreement contains any substantial errors, always retype completely that entire page.)

When you run down the contents of your final draft and carefully compare the items to be sure that the contents reflect exactly what both parties intend to provide, ask yourselves (both of you) these questions: Did we get everything? Is there anything we might like to adjust or add in the final draft? Is my intent and my spouse's and the language of the Agreement — every sentence, paragraph—clear and unambiguous? Counter-check and make the necessary adjustments, accordingly. And if there have been any further corrections, then type (or write) out a final, perfect copy.

IT'S NOW DONE. The next order of business is the "execution" phase — the SIGNING AND WITNESSING of the Agreement you've just finished drafting. For that, turn to Chapter 7 at p. 62 for the procedures.

Sample 1: Married Couple With Minor Children, Substantial Premarital Property, And Some Pension Rights.

MARITAL SEPARATION/SETTLEMENT AGREEMENT

(A Sample)

THIS AGREEMENT is made on the date hereinafter entered below, between Mr. _________________, residing at ______________ (hereinafter referred to as "HUSBAND"); and Mrs. _______________, residing at _______________ (hereinafter referred to as "WIFE"),

RECITALS

WITNESSETH:

1. The parties were married on the ______ day of _______, 19__, in the City of _____, County/Parish of _______, State of ________, and the said marriage persists to this date.

2. As a result of the disputes and unfortunate differences which have developed between the parties, they separated *(OR, they propose to separate shortly hereafter)* on or about the ___ day of _________ 19__, and will live separate and apart at all times thereafter.

3. There have developed some unfortunate disputes and irreconcilable differences between the parties which make further living together as man and wife or continuation of the marriage impracticable; and in mutual recognition of this, the parties do desire to, and by this agreement intend to, settle all marital issues, property rights, legal entitlements and obligations which may exist between them in consequence of the marital relationship, and, particularly, to do so in a peaceful, mature, civilized, and amicable manner as free of bitterness as practicable.

4. Both parties expressly acknowledge that they respectively have the opportunity to, and that they are fully aware that they have the right to, seek individual legal counsel or representation in the making of this agreement, if they so choose or prefer; but the parties, in the exercise of their adult right to choose, have by their own free will chosen to act for and by themselves herein.

5. ***Financial Condition.*** The husband and wife have each submitted to the other a financial Statement of Networth as of the _______ day of ________, 19__, and each party herewith acknowledges receipt of same; and each represents to the other that the assets and liabilities reflected in the said statements are an accurate and true picture of his or her financial condition. The said net worth statement is attached hereto as Exhibit "A", and each is counter-signed and dated by the other to indicate his or her acknowledgment of receipt of same. [NOTE: Parties must be sure to actually exchange and attach this statement before or at the actual execution date, and to counter sign and date each statement showing the date of the exchange]

6. ***Statistical Information.*** The Husband's social security number is ______________
The Wife's social security number is ________________.

7. The names and birth dates of the minor children born (or legally adopted) of this marriage, are: (If no children, enter: NONE)

I. ______________________ IV. ______________________
II. ______________________ V. ______________________
III. ______________________ VI. ______________________

NOW, THEREFORE, in consideration of the promises and mutual agreements, covenants and undertakings contained herein, and for good and valuable consideration, the parties mutually agree as follows:

PART I
SEPARATION AGREEMENT

ARTICLE I: Separation and Non-molestation

From and after the signing of this agreement, both parties may, and shall at all times hereinafter, live and/or continue to live separate and apart from each other; and each shall be free from the interference, authority and control, direct or indirect, of the other as fully as if each party were single and unmarried to the other. Each shall be at liberty to act and to do as he or she sees fit and proper, and to conduct his or her personal and social life and associations as freely and as fully as if he or she were single and unmarried to each other.

ARTICLE 2: Child Custody

(Pick Paragraph A or B, as applicable to you)

A. ***One party with primary custody —The other with visitation rights***

The parties agree that *Husband/Wife** , shall have custody and control of the minor child(ren) of the marriage; it would be in the best interests of, and would best promote the welfare of, the minor children that the *(Husband/Wife)* have reasonable visitation rights with the minor children away from the custodial home at the following times: *(Enter agreed provisions, as in "Sample Visitation Guidelines" on p. 21).*

Example: (1) Every other weekend from _________ to ___________ p.m. on Fridays, until ___________ p.m. on Sunday;

(2) Two periods of seven consecutive days during the summer each year;
(3) On Father's Day from ___________ to ___________ p.m.;
(4) On Mother's Day from ___________ to ___________ p.m.;
(5) On Easter, Christmas, and Thanksgiving from ___________ p.m. until ___________ p.m.
(6) On the children's birthdays from ___________ p.m. until ___________ p.m.
(7) Every other week from ___________ p.m. on Friday until ___________ p.m. on Friday of the following week;
(8) At such other times as are mutually agreed to between the parties.

The parties agree that visitation is highly encouraged, but is optional. The non-custodial parent shall give at least forty-eight (48) hours advance notice if unable to exercise a scheduled visitation period.

B. ***Joint custody by both parties***

The parties agree that the Husband an Wife each desire to have and maintain the privilege and responsibility of the custody for their minor child(ren). Therefore, the parties agree to joint custody of the minor child(ren), and each party shall share the privilege and responsibility for the custody and control of the minor children. The primary right

* Strike out one or the other, as is necessary.

and responsibility to supervise and control the custody and upbringing of the children shall be with the parent with whom the children are residing at any given time. *The parties agree that the children shall reside with the Husband at the following times: (enter applicable provisions, as in paragraph A above, for example).*

And the parties agree that the children shall reside with the Wife at the following times: *(enter applicable provisions, as in paragraph A above, for example).*

C. Neither party to alienate child(ren) from the other.

(1) Each of the parties shall take all measures deemed advisable to foster a feeling of affection between the child(ren) and the other party, and neither party shall do anything which may estrange the child(ren) from the other party or impair the child(ren)'s high regard for the other party.

(2) *Parties to confer on important matters*

The parties shall confer with each other on all important matters pertaining to the child(ren)'s health, welfare, education, an upbringing, with a view toward arriving at a harmonious policy calculated to promote the child(ren)'s best interests.

(3) *Notification in event of illness*

Each party shall promptly notify the other in the event of the illness of any child residing with him or her. During such illness, the other party shall have the right to visit the child at reasonable times for reasonable periods.

(4) *Equal access to records*

Each party shall have access to all school and medical records and reports of the child(ren).

(5) *Right to be appointed guardian*

Nothing in this agreement shall be deemed to be a waiver by either party, if he or she is the surviving parent, of his or her right to be appointed guardian of the person and property (or either) of the minor child(ren).

(6) *Travel restrictions*

Neither party shall take the child(ren) outside the boundaries of the continental United States without the consent of the other party, and each party agrees to notify the other at least sixty (60) days in advance before changing their permanent residence outside the county of _______, State of _________ .

(7) *Proper forum to determine custody matters*

The parties agree that the _________ County, State of ________, is the proper forum to determine any changes of custody and each agrees to be bound jurisdictionally to a custody determination in the said county, if that should ever be necessary.

ARTICLE 3: Child Support

(1) *Husband/Wife to make monthly payment*

The *(Husband/Wife)** shall provide as child support for the benefit of the child(ren), and will pay to the *(Husband/Wife)*, the sum of $_____ (same in words: _________) per month, per child. These child support payments shall be made on or before the first day of each month following the execution of this agreement, and shall continue until the first to happen of the following events:

(1) Either husband or wife dies; or
(2) Upon the death of the child for which support is being paid; or

---

* In all instances, strike out one or the other, as is necessary

(3) Upon a child reaching his or her eighteenth birthday; or
(4) Upon the marriage of a child; or
(5) Upon the child permanently deserting the home; or
(6) Pursuant to an order of a court of competent jurisdiction.

(2) The parties agree that the designated paying party's estate shall have no obligation for the unaccrued child support payments upon the party's death.

[Or, If appropriate, change last sentence to the following: "the parties agree that the (Husband's/Wife's) obligation to pay child support shall be an obligation of (his/her) estate and shall be binding upon the heirs, executors, and administrators to the extent and for such period as the child for whom support is being paid shall continue to be entitled to such payment after (Husband's/Wife's) death"].*

(3) *Will Equally support Children —no payment in joint custody*

The parties acknowledge that they desire that their child(ren) be adequately supported. The parties have agreed to a joint custody arrangement whereby each party has the minor child(ren) for an equal amount of time each month; therefore, each party agrees to equally share the costs of supporting the minor child(ren), and neither party shall be required to pay the other any amount for the support of the minor child(ren).

(4) *Schedule for increased child support payments*

The monthly payments for child support shall be increased according to the following schedule:

(1) Upon the attainment of the __________ birthday, to $________ per month;
(2) Upon the attainment of the __________ birthday, to $________ per month;

(Add additional paragraphs for each increase).

(5) *Adjustments based upon changed circumstances*

The sum herein agreed to be paid by the *(Husband/ Wife)* to the *(Husband/Wife)* for child support shall be subject to change in accordance with the changed circumstances of the parties. In the event the circumstances of either party do change and the parties are unable to agree upon the amount thereafter to be paid, the party desiring the change may submit the question to a court of competent jurisdiction and both parties shall be bound by the determination of the said court.

(6) *Continuation of support during college*

If any child of the parties shall be enrolled in college on or before his/her twentieth birthday, then the payments specified in this agreement for the support for such child shall be continued beyond such child's eighteenth birthday until such child completes (his/her) undergraduate education and earns an academic degree or withdraws from college.

(7) *Payment of costs for undergraduate college education*

If any child of the parties should decide to pursue an undergraduate education, the *(Husband/Wife)* agrees to pay all [or, if more appropriate, then enter: One-Half] the costs of tuition, room and board, to the extent such costs are not covered by scholarships, for the attendance by such child at the college or other institution of higher education as shall be mutually selected by the parties, such selection to be made in keeping with the economic means of both parties. The *(Husband/Wife)* agrees to pay such costs so long as each child is continuing his/her education in good faith, with at least average grades, and with reasonable progress toward an undergraduate degree.

(8) *Health insurance for children*

The child(ren) are presently covered by medical and hospital insurance and the *(Husband/Wife)* shall maintain such insurance for the benefit of the minor child(ren) and shall pay the premiums thereon in addition to other support

---

* In all instances, strike out <u>one</u> or the other, as is necessary

payments as provided in this agreement. In the event any part of the insurance is canceled, then *(Husband/Wife)* shall procure a substantially similar insurance coverage for the minor child(ren). In addition, the *(Husband/Wife)* shall be responsible for all (or one-half of all) reasonable and necessary medical dental and drug expenses for the minor child(ren) which are not covered by insurance.

(9) *Life Insurance for children*
*(Husband/Wife)** shall maintain in good standing with a reputable company a separate insurance policy on (his/her) life for the benefit of each minor child of the parties so long as such child is entitled to support under the terms of this agreement, in the face amount of not less than __________ Dollars ($__________); such insurance shall be payable to each respective child as a beneficiary, and when received by or for the said child shall be in full satisfaction and settlement of any obligation for support of the child by the *(Husband/Wife)* or *(his/her)* estate after the said *(Husband's/Wife's)* death.

ARTICLE 4: Alimony/Maintenance

(1) *Waiver of Alimony*
The husband and wife acknowledge that neither shall pay to the other, nor make any claim, for alimony, support and maintenance against the other under the laws of the State of _________ or of any other state. Wherefore, the parties herein waive and release any and all rights that may exist against the other in this regard, and the parties acknowledge that this release and waiver is independent of any other provisions of this agreement.

OR:

(2) *Monthly alimony payment*
The *(Husband/Wife)* agrees to pay as alimony to the *(Husband/Wife)* the sum of $______ per month. These alimony payments shall be made on or before the first day of the month following the execution of this agreement, and shall continue until the first to happen of the following events:

(1) *(Husband/Wife/the Beneficiary)* remarries; or
(2) ________ years have elapsed since the signing of this agreement; or
(3) Either Husband or Wife dies; or
(4) (Husband/Wife/the beneficiary) becomes disabled so that (he/she) is unable to work, then during that period of disability.

(3) The parties agree that the *(Husband's/Wife's)* estate shall have no obligation for the *(Husband's/Wife's)* support.

[Or, alternatively, if more appropriate, then change this last sentence to the following: ' The parties agree that *(Husband's/Wife's)* obligation to support *(Husband/Wife)* shall be an obligation of (his/her) estate and shall be binding upon the heirs, executors and administrators of the estate to the extent and for such period as the *(Husband's/Wife's)* shall continue to be entitled to such payment after *(Husband's/Wife's death*'.]

(4) *Health insurance for dependent spouse*
By way of further support and maintenance for *(Husband/Wife)*, and for so long as *(Husband/Wife)* shall be required to pay alimony as provided in paragraph 2 and 3 above, *(Husband/Wife)* shall be fully responsible, either directly or through insurance provided and maintained by *(him/her)*, for all reasonably necessary medical, dental, or drug expenses incurred by *(Husband/Wife)*.

---

* In all instances, strike out one or the other, as is necessary

(5) *Life Insurance for dependent spouse*
(Husband/Wife) agrees to maintain life insurance coverage for the benefit of the *(Husband/Wife)* at least in the amount of $________, which designates (him/her) as sole beneficiary. The *(Husband/Wife)* agrees to advise the *(Husband/Wife)* of the policy number of the insurance policy or policies and agrees to execute the appropriate documents with the appropriate company or companies irrevocably designating the *(Husband/Wife** *)* as the sole beneficiary. The *(Husband/Wife)* further agrees to keep the policy or policies in full force and effect by maintaining the premiums thereon. In the event the insurance proceeds payable to *(Husband/Wife)* at the *(Husband's/Wife's)* death are not equal to the amount provided herein, then the *(Husband/Wife)* shall have a valid claim or charge against the *(Husband's/Wife's)** estate for the amount of the difference.

(6) ***Alimony limitation provision***
The party receiving alimony payment under this agreement, is any, namely the *(Husband/Wife),* acknowledges that the benefits accruing to *(him/her)* under and by virtue of this agreement as alimony and/or support and maintenance, are reasonable and adequate, and (he/she) expressly waives all claims against the *(Husband/Wife)* for further alimony, support and maintenance except as herein provided.

(7) ***Modification of alimony provision***
The provisions for alimony, support and maintenance of the *(husband/Wife)* , as provided herein, if any, are fixed payments, and shall not be modified or changed, except by further agreement of the parties expressed in writing.

(8) ***Nonintegration of alimony provision***
The provisions for alimony, support and maintenance of the *(Husband/Wife)* in this agreement, if any, are independent of any provision or agreement for division of property between the parties, and such provisions shall not for any purpose be deemed a part of or merged in or integrated with a property settlement of the parties.

PART II
PROPERTY SETTLEMENT

ARTICLE 5: Family Residence

Family Residence
(1) The parties at the present time are owners, as tenants by the entirety, of a house and lot located at*: (state address, including town, state*), which was formerly used by the parties as their family residence.

Option I: *Conveyance of family residence to one spouse*
(2) Simultaneously with the execution of this agreement, the *(Husband/Wife)* shall execute a general warranty deed transferring *(his/her)* interest in the property to the (*Husband/Wife),* and the *(Husband/Wife*) agrees to assume and be solely responsible for all future mortgage payments to ______________ *(name of lender)***.** In addition, the *(Husband/Wife)*agrees to be solely responsible for all ad valorem property taxes, assessments, insurance, and all maintenance and repairs pertaining to said property and agrees to hold the *(Husband/Wife)* harmless from any liability in this regard and to indemnify (him/her) if (he/she) should ever be caused to make any payment in this regard.

* In all instances, strike out one or the other, as is necessary

Option II: *Ownership converted to tenancy in common*
(3) It is agreed that following the execution of this agreement, the family residence shall be owned by the parties as tenants in common.

Option III: *Use by (Husband/Wife*) until divorce*
(4) *The (Husband/Wife)** **shall be entitled to occupy and use the family residence, without payment of rent to** *(Husband/Wife),* **until such time as the parties shall obtain an absolute divorce.**

Option IV: *Use by (Husband/Wife) until remarriage*
(5) *(Husband/Wife)* **shall be entitled to occupy and use the family residence, without payment of rent to** *(Husband/Wife).* **for so long as** *(he/she)* **shall remain unmarried.**

Option V: *Use by (Husband/Wife) so long as children reside there, or until youngest child reaches age 21*
(6) *(Husband/Wife)* **shall be entitled to occupy and use the family residence, without payment of rent to** *(Husband/Wife)*, **until the children of the marriage no longer make the residence their home, or until the youngest child shall reach age twenty-one (21), whichever should first occur.**

Option VI: *Family residence sold and the proceeds divided*
(7) Promptly following the execution of this agreement, the said family residence shall be sold and the proceeds shall be equally divided between Husband and Wife.

Payment of mortgage and expenses during occupancy period
(8) During the period of occupancy of the family residence by the *(Husband/Wife),* **the** *(Husband/Wife)* **shall pay all of the mortgage payments to ______________** *(Name of Lender),* **and all [or, if more applicable: ONE-HALF] of the payments in ad valorem taxes, assessments, insurance, and major repairs pertaining to the property, the term "major repairs" being defined as any costs in connection with repair or replacement of the water heater, air conditioner, furnace, plumbing, roof, structural damage to walls, floors or ceiling, or exterior painting, costing over fifty ($50.00) dollars. This obligation shall not extend to any repair costs which are covered by insurance.**

Such payments in addition to other support in agreement
(9) Such payments by the *(Husband/Wife)* **under this paragraph shall be in addition to other payments for the support and maintenance of the** *(Husband/Wife)* **and the minor children otherwise provided for in this agreement, if any.**

ARTICLE 6: Motor Vehicles

Motor Vehicles
(1) *Acknowledgment of sole ownership and assumption of debt*
The parties agree that the *(Husband/Wife)* shall have as *(his/her)* **sole and separate property the** *(make and model of motor vehicle)* **presently titled in** *(his/her)* **name, and** *(he/she)* **shall assume as (his/her) sole and separate obligation the outstanding indebtedness owed on said motor vehicle to** *(name of lender)***.**

(2) *Acknowledgment of sole ownership — with no assumption of debt*
The parties agree that *(Husband/Wife)* **shall have as (his/her) sole and separate property the** *(make and model of motor vehicle)* **presently titled in (his/her) name which is unencumbered.**

---

* In all instances, strike out <u>one</u> or the other, as is necessary

(3) *Agreement to convey ownership with assumption of debt*
The *(Husband/Wife*)* agrees to convey to the *(Husband/Wife*)* all rights, title, and interest which (he/she) has in the *(make and model of motor vehicle),* and the *(Husband/Wife*)* shall assume as (his/hers) sole and separate obligation the outstanding indebtedness owed on vehicle to *(name of lender)*. [Or, 'the said vehicle is fully paid for and will be conveyed free of any liens or encumbrances to Husband/Wife'].

[Additional paragraphs using the above or similar language, may be used to cover all motor vehicles owned by the parties, if applicable].

ARTICLE 7: Life Insurance

Life Insurance Policies
The following policies of insurance on the life of the *(Husband/Wife)* are in force and effect:
(1) Policy No. ______________ issued by ___________________________ in the face amount of $__________
(Add additional subparagraphs for each policy, if more policies apply.) It is agreed that each policy shall be assigned to the *(Husband/Wife)* as *(his/hers)* sole and separate property.

ARTICLE 8: Joint Accounts

Acknowledgment of ownership
The parties own the following joint accounts which are held in both names:

Name & Address of Bank	Account No.	Current Balance

Immediately following the signing of this agreement, each account shall be closed out and the total proceeds, thereof, divided and paid as follows to the parties: ____ percentage to the Husband, and ____ percentage to the Wife.

ARTICLE 9: Personal Property

Ownership in property listed on Schedule "B" to the (Husband/Wife)
1. The _____*(Husband/Wife)*____) shall have as his/her sole and separate property, all of the items of personal property listed in Schedule "B", which is hereto attached and signed by the parties and is herewith incorporated to this agreement by reference.
[If it applies, make additional paragraphs with a separate schedule, say Schedule "C", for property to be assigned to the other spouse]

Previously divided property and waiver of future claims
The parties agree that, except as otherwise stipulated in the agreement, the furniture, household furnishing, and all other personal property acquired by them during the marriage or contributed to the marital property, has been divided in a mutually agreeable fashion between them, and neither party shall henceforth lay any claims to such property now in the hands of the other.

---

* In all instances, strike out one or the other, as is necessary

ARTICLE 10: Debts

A. *List of debts to be paid by the Husband*

It is agreed that the Husband shall pay the following existing debts of the parties which accrued from the marriage:

Name and Address of Creditor	Account No.	Principal Balance

B. *List of debts to be paid by the Wife*

It is agreed that the Wife shall pay the following existing debts of the parties which accrued from the marriage: [*Specify the same details and information as in part A above. if applicable*]

C. The Husband an the Wife each agrees to hold the other harmless and to indemnify each other, if applicable, if any should be caused to make any payment other than as provided above. Husband and Wife represent and warrant, each to the other, that they have not heretofore incurred any debt or made any commitment for which the other party or his or her estate may be liable, except as otherwise noted in this agreement. Both parties hereby covenant that they will not at any time following the execution of this agreement contract any debts, charges or liabilities whatsoever for which the other party or his or her property or estate shall become personally liable or answerable.

ARTICLE 11: Mutual Release of Property/Inheritance Rights

A. Waiver of Claims

Except as otherwise provided in this agreement, the Husband and the Wife do hereby waive, release, discharge, quitclaim and renounce each to the other, and to their respective heirs and assigns, all rights to claim an equal or equitable distribution of property or distributive award pursuant to the laws of this state or any state, and/or, all rights to a share in the estate upon the death of the other, and/or all rights to elect to take a life estate upon the death of the other, and/or all rights to take under or dissent from the will of the other, and/or all rights to act as administrator or executor of the other's estate, and/or any and all other rights which either party may now have, or may hereafter acquire, under the present or future laws of any jurisdiction arising out of the marital relationship.

B. *Release of all rights except suit for uncontested divorce*

Each party releases and discharges the other from all causes of action, claims, rights or demands in law or equity, which either party may now have, or may hereafter acquire against the other under the present or future laws of any jurisdiction, except any and all causes of action for divorce based on any legal ground for divorce that might exist in any jurisdiction in which either party may become a resident.

C. *Release of property rights*

Except as otherwise provided herein, the Husband and Wife do herewith grant, release and forever quitclaim to each other all right, title, interest, claim an demand whatsoever in the real property which the other now owns or may hereafter acquire, and each party may hereafter purchase, acquire, own, hold, possess, encumber, dispose of and convey any and all classes and kinds of real and personal property as though unmarried, free from the consent, joinder, and interference of the other party. Each party agrees that, hereafter, in the sale or transfer and conveyance of any property, real or personal, it shall not be necessary that the other party sign the deed, deed of trust, mortgage, or bill of sale or any other documents(s)conveying the property, for the grantee or purchaser to have a good title.

PART III
ARTICLE 12: Qualified Domestic Relations Order Provisions

Qualified Domestic Relations Order [QDRO]*

[Applies only in a marital situation in which pension rights are involved]

Defendant currently has certain rights and benefits in a qualified employee retirement plan maintained by his employer, *[enter the company name]*. This order is intended to be a Qualified Domestic Relations Order [or QDRO, for Short] within the meaning of Section 206(d) of the Employee Retirement Income Security Act of 1974 and Section 414 (p) of the Internal Revenue Code of 1954, both as amended by the Retirement Equity Act of 1984. *For purposes of this Order Defendant and Plaintiff state and agree as follows:*

a. This paragraph and the order shall apply to the following employee Plan: *[enter name of the plan]* ("the Plan")

b. It is stipulated that as of [date], the total vested amounts credited to Defendant's Profit Sharing Plan was $*[vested amounts]* and that Defendant's rights to benefits under the Plan as of the day of divorce, constitutes marital property.

c. The Participant in the applicable qualified Plan is *[employed spouse's name]* ("Participant") whose last known mailing address is ________________ and his/her Social Security Number is ____________.

d. *[Non-pensioned spouse's name]*, spouse of the participant, shall for purposes of this paragraph be referred to as the "Alternate Payee." The last known mailing address for the Alternate Payee is ____________________ and his/her Social Security Number is __________________.

e. "Earliest Retirement Age" means the earliest date on which, under the Plans, the Participant could elect to receive benefits.

f. Immediately upon the receipt of a copy of this order, the Trustee or Administrator of the Plan shall establish a separate account under the Plan for the benefit of the Alternate Payee and transfer to such account for the Plan a portion of the Participant's account balance in the Pension Plan equal to $ [*non-employee spouse's share of the plan*] plus all Plan earnings, except for employer contributions, since *dates*. The Trustee shall create and hold this account for the exclusive benefit of the Alternate Payee. Throughout the time the Trustee is required to maintain the said account, the Trustee shall continue to allocate and contribute to the Alternate Payee's account its proportionate share of plan earnings as called for under the Plan. However, the Trustee shall not contribute or allocate to the account any portion of future employer contribution to the Plans. At all times that the Trustee is holding all or any portion of the account, the Alternate Payee shall for all purposes be treated as a beneficiary of the Plan and to the extent provided for in the Internal Revenue Code of 1954 and the Employee Retirement Income Security Act of 1974, as each may be amended, and he/she shall have all rights and benefits accorded to the Participant under the Plan. In the event of the Participant's death prior to attaining the age at which benefits are payable to him, the Alternate Payee shall be treated as his beneficiary entitled to receive payment of the Alternate Payee's account as a death benefit under the Plan.

---

* NOTE: Note that QDRO does not apply (is not necessary) under the distribution option where the parties divide the benefits so that the pension participant (the employee spouse) keeps the full benefits in exchange for the other spouse receiving some other assets. Nor is QDRO required for dividing military retirement pay. QDRO is ONLY required (it only applies) in the distribution option where the non-employee spouse is given the right to receive part of the retirement benefits at a somewhat later date, namely when those benefits are eventually paid out upon the participant's retirement. And then it applies only to "defined benefit" and "defined contribution" plans like 401(K) and profit sharing plans — and not to Individual Retirement Accounts.

Hence, unless such options and plans apply in your case, simply exclude this whole Article 12. (See Chap. 3 at pp 16-17, and Appendix B at pp. 91, for more on this)

g. The Participant shall not borrow against the pension assets, except with the written consent and approval of the Alternate Payee.

h. The Alternate Payee shall be entitled to elect, in the manner provided for under the Plan, to receive or commence to receive distribution of the amount credited to her account at any time after the Participant has attained the earliest retirement age, whether or not Participant has retired or separated from service. The Alternate Payee shall be allowed to elect any form of payment available under the Plan, but shall not be entitled to any form of payment which would not be allowed the Participant. Such payments to the Alternate Payee shall be available for the entire period during which the Participant, *[his/her name]*, is entitled to benefits under the Plan.

i. This paragraph shall be binding upon any successor plan maintained by the employer, *[employer's name]*, or its successor. Participant and Alternative Payee agree that the terms of this paragraph will be construed, and if necessary, amended so as to qualify as a Qualified Domestic Relations Order.

PART IV
ARTICLE 13: GENERAL PROVISIONS

Tax Returns and Exemptions

A. *Joint Tax Returns—(Husband/Wife)* to pay tax, own refund*

If requested by the *(Husband/Wife),** the *(Husband/Wife)** agrees to execute and file joint tax returns, both federal and state, for the calendar year 19__ *[enter the last year of joint returns]*. The *(Husband/Wife)* * agrees to be liable for all taxes, penalties, fines, an other assessments which might have to be paid for those years in which the parties filed or may file joint tax returns. The parties agree that any income tax refunds shall be *(equally divided)*** or (*shall be the sole and separate property of the (husband/Wife),*** and the *(Husband/Wife),** and the *(Husband/Wife)** agrees to furnish (his/her) endorsement on any tax refund check upon the request of the *(Husband/Wife).**

B. *Dependency exemptions allocated to one spouse only*

i. The parties agree that the *(Husband/Wife)* is entitled to claim any dependency exemptions or deductions that may be allowed on the Federal and State income tax returns for the following children ____________________ for the years and for as long as (he/she) complies with the child support provisions of this agreement or any supplemental agreements between the parties. At the request of the *(Husband/Wife),** the *(Husband/Wife)** shall execute such written declaration as may be required for tax purposes to indicate (his/her) intention not to claim the dependency exceptions or deductions that may be allowed.

Dependency exemption split

OR ii. The parties agree that the dependency exemption or deduction that may be allowed on the Federal and State income tax returns shall be divided between them as follows:

(1) Husband shall be entitled to the dependency exemption or deduction for *[names of the intended children]*, and Wife hereby expressly waives such dependency exemption or deduction in connection with such child(ren).

(2) Wife shall be entitled to the dependency exemption or deduction for *[names of the intended children]*, and Husband hereby expressly waives such dependency exemption or deduction in connection with such child(ren).

---

* In all instances, strike out one or the other word, as is necessary

At the request of either spouse, the other spouse shall execute such written declaration as may be required for tax purposes to indicate (his/her) intention not to claim the dependency exemptions or deductions that may be allowed.

ARTICLE 14

Enforcement of Agreement

In the event that a dispute should arise over the interpretation, fulfillment or specific performance of any clauses in this agreement, the matter shall be submitted to arbitration to be resolved, and the following person(s) or institution(s) are hereby appointed to act as the arbitrator(s) in such matters: *(You may designate, by name, one or more priests, pastors or rabbis, mutual friends, or say The American Arbitration Association)*. Any decisions made on the disputed issues by such arbitrators (or by a court to which the parties shall still retain the rights to resort to) shall be final for both parties. The costs and expenses incurred for arbitration, or otherwise incurred for enforcing or litigating the disputed matters in a court of law, shall be borne solely by the party who is found to be at fault.

ARTICLE 15

Incorporation into Divorce Judgment, Survival of Agreement

This Agreement shall in no way be construed as a consent to, or collusion to bring about a divorce or dissolution of marriage on the part of the parties. In the event, however, that one party (or both) sooner or later brings an action for a divorce or dissolution of marriage in a court of competent jurisdiction in a State wherein either party resides, the parties agree that the provisions of this agreement shall be binding and controlling, and be deemed the complete settlement of all marital issues between the parties, and that the said provisions of this agreement shall further be incorporated, in full and in substance, into the resultant Judgment of Divorce or Dissolution, by reference. This Agreement shall not be merged into any such judgment of divorce or dissolution, but shall survive and be separately binding on the parties.

ARTICLE 16

Voluntary Execution and Acceptance of Competence of the Parties

Both parties hereby state that they are of full age and sufficient education and intelligence, and that they have read and considered the provisions and implications of this agreement and completely understand and agree with same. They acknowledge that they have negotiated and entered into this agreement totally of their own free will and volition, and that no undue influence, coercion, pressure or force has been used by or against either party in the negotiation, signings and acceptance of this agreement, either by the other party or by any other persons. The parties acknowledge that the provisions of this agreement are fair, adequate and satisfactory to each of them.

ARTICLE 17

Modification and Waiver

Except as otherwise provided herein, this agreement may be modified or amended only by agreement of the parties, in writing, and executed with the same formality as this agreement. The failure of either party to insist upon a strict performance of any provision of this agreement shall not constitute a waiver of any subsequent default of the same or similar nature.

ARTICLE 18

Severability of Agreement

It is agreed that each paragraph of this agreement has been separately and individually agreed upon and contracted for by and between the parties, and if any paragraph of this agreement or any subsection hereof is held to be invalid or unenforceable, it shall have no effect on the remainder of the agreement but said agreement shall remain and continue in full force and effect.

ARTICLE 19

Additional Instruments

Each party shall from time to time, at the request of the other execute, acknowledge and deliver to the other party all further documents and instruments that may be reasonably required to give full force and effect to the provisions of this agreement.

ARTICLE 20

Binding Effect and Entire Agreement

This agreement contains the entire understanding of the parties, and there are no representations, warranties, covenants, or undertakings other than those expressed and set forth herein. Except as otherwise stated in this agreement, all provisions in this agreement shall be binding upon the respective heirs, next of kin, executors, administrators, trustees, and all legal representatives of the parties.

ARTICLE 21

Governing Law

This agreement shall be construed in accordance with, and governed by, the laws of the State of ______________ regardless of the forum where it may come up for construction.

IN WITNESS WHEREOF, the parties hereby voluntarily sign, seal and acknowledge this agreement in duplicate originals, one of which is retained by each of the parties hereto, this____ day of ____________, 19__.

SIGNED: ________________________________ ________________________
(Husband) (Date of Signing)

Present Address: ____

____

SIGNED: ________________________________ ________________________
(Wife) (Date of Signing)

Present Address: ____

____

VERIFICATION

STATE OF ______________:
COUNTY OF _____________: SS.

On this date, the ____day of ________. 19__, before me, a Notary Public in and for the State and County captioned above, personally appeared Mr. ________________________, personally known or made known to me to be the person who executed the foregoing SEPARATION/SETTLEMENT Agreement, and the said person stated under oath under penalties of perjury, that the facts and statements contained in this document are true and that he freely and voluntarily executed the said agreement for the purposes named therein.

WITNESS my hand and seal.

____
(Notary Stamp/Signature)

STATE OF _____________:
COUNTY OF ____________: SS.

On this date, the ____day of ___________ 19__, before me, a Notary Public in and for the State and County captioned above, personally appeared Mrs. ____________________, personally known or made known to me to be the person who executed the foregoing SEPARATION/SETTLEMENT Agreement, and the said person stated under oath under penalties of perjury, that the facts and statements contained in this document are true and that she freely and voluntarily executed the said agreement for the purposes named therein.

WITNESS my hand and seal.

____
(Notary Stamp/Signature)

CERTIFICATION BY SUBSCRIBING WITNESSES TO AGREEMENT

We, the undersigned witness(es) whose names are hereunto subscribed, DO HEREBY CERTIFY under the penalty of perjury, that on the ______________ day of ____________ 19__, both of the parties above named, respectively signed their names to this instrument in our presence and in the presence of each of us and at the same time, in our presence and to our hearing, the said persons declared the same to be their Written Agreement, made by and freely agreed to by them, and requested us and each of us, to sign our names thereto as witnesses to the execution thereof, which we hereby do in the presence of the parties and of each other, on the day of the date of the said execution. The said parties appeared to be under no duress, force, compulsion or constraint of any kind when they signed the said agreement.

SIGNED:

(1) ____________________________ of ____________________________________
(Signature and Name) (Address)

(2) ____________________________ of ____________________________________
(Signature and Name) (Address)

(3) ____________________________ of ____________________________________
(Signature and Name) (Address)

SAMPLE 2: Married Couple With NO Children, Little Or No Property, And No Pension Rights

MARITAL SEPARATION/SETTLEMENT AGREEMENT
(A SAMPLE)

THIS AGREEMENT is made on the date hereinafter entered below, between Mr. ______________ residing at ____________________ (hereinafter referred to as "Husband"); and Mrs. ______________ residing at __________________ (hereinafter referred to as "Wife"), *WITNESSETH:*

RECITALS

1. The parties were married on the _____ day of _____, 19__, in the City of _____________, County/Parish of ________, State of ____, and the said marriage persists to this date.

2. As a result of the disputes and unfortunate differences which have developed between the parties, they separated (OR, *they propose to separate shortly hereafter*) on or about the ____day of _______ 19 __, and will live separate and apart at all times thereafter.

3. There have developed some unfortunate disputes and irreconcilable differences between the parties which make further living together as man and wife or continuation of the marriage impracticable; and in mutual recognition of this the parties as desire to, and by this agreement intend to, settle all marital issues, property rights, legal claims, entitlements and obligations which may exist between them in consequence of the marital relationship, and, particularly, to do so in a peaceful, mature, civilized, and amicable manner as free of bitterness as practicable.

4. Both parties expressly acknowledge that they respectively have the opportunity to, and that they are fully aware that they have the right to, seek individual legal counsel or representation in the making of this agreement, if they so choose or prefer; but the parties, in the exercise of their adult right to choose, have by their own free will chosen to act for and by themselves herein.

5. *Financial Condition.* The husband and wife have each submitted to the other a Statement of New Worth as of _______ day of _______ 19___, and each party herewith acknowledges the receipt of same; and each represents to the other that the assets and liabilities reflected in the said statement are accurate and true picture of his or her financial condition. The said net worth statement is attached hereto as Exhibit "A", and each is counter-signed and dated by the other to indicate his or her receipt of same. [NOTE: Parties must be sure to actually exchange and

*NOTE: Whenever there is the term "Husband/Wife," enter only one or the other — i.e., either "Husband" or "Wife," as is appropriate, and strike out the other word

attach this statement before or at the actual execution date, and to counter-sign and date each statement showing the date of the exchange.]

6. *Statistical Information.* The Husband's social security number is ________________. The Wife's social security number is ______________________.

NOW THEREFORE, in consideration of the promises and mutual agreements, covenants and undertakings contained herein, and for good and valuable consideration, the parties mutually agree as follows:

7. From and after the signing of this agreement, both parties may, and shall at all times hereinafter, live and/or continue to live separate and apart from each other; and each shall be free from the interference, authority and control, direct or indirect, of the other as fully as if each party were single and unmarried to the other. Each shall be at liberty to act and to do as he or she sees fit and proper, and to conduct his or her personal and social life as freely and associations as fully as if he or she were single and unmarred to each other.

8. There are no minor child(ren) born of (and /or adopted in) the marriage, who are under the age of 18 (or 21).

9. *Joint Tax Returns -- (Husband/Wife)* to pay tax, own refund*
If requested by the *(Husband/Wife),* * the (husband/wife) agrees to execute and file joint tax returns for the calendar year 19__ and all other years permitted by law. *(Husband/Wife)* agrees to be liable for all taxes, penalties, fines, and other assessments which might have to be paid for those years in which the parties filed or may file joint tax returns. The parties agree that any income tax refunds shall be *(equally divided) (shall be the sole and separate property of the Husband/Wife),* and *(Husband/Wife)* agrees to furnish (his/her) endorsement on any tax refund check upon the request of *(Husband/Wife).*

10a. The parties hereby stipulate and declare the property listed below to be the *complete* MARITAL AND/OR COMMUNITY PROPERTY of the parties now existing which have not yet been distributed by an between them, if any: ______________________________________.

10b. The said undistributed marital and/or community property shall be distributed between the parties in the manner set forth below, which distribution is hereby agreed and deemed by both parties to be fair and equitable:

______________________________________.

OR:** **11.** The PARTIES have already divided and distributed among themselves any and all MARITAL and/or COMMUNITY PROPERTY owned by them to each other's complete and mutual satisfaction. Except as otherwise expressly set forth in Paragraphs 10a and 10b above, if any, any and all items of property or asset of whatever kind or description and wherever located, whether real or personal property or otherwise, which is in the name of, or possessed by or under the control of or otherwise owned by either party, are herewith deemed and declared to be SEPARATE PROPERTY of each such party, solely owned now and at all times hereafter in all respects by the party having his/her name on the property, or having possession or control thereto.

12. The Husband and Wife herein hereby waive alimony, maintenance or financial support or entitlement of any kind or description, and any and all rights thereto to seek or receive same at any time; it is mutually concurred that the parties have been, and are now self-supporting and/or capable of supporting themselves.

13. Each Party stipulates that there are no substantial marital debts currently outstanding which are JOINT obligations of the parties. In the event that there are such existing, the parties agree that they shall be assumed and

---

* NOTE: Whenever there is the term "Husband/Wife," enter only one or the other — i.e., either "Husband" or "Wife," as is appropriate, and strike out the other word

** If no marital property is applicable to you or is in dispute, enter 'NONE" in paragraphs 10a and b, and leave paragraph 11 'as is.'

paid off by the parties as follows: (*specify the names and addresses of creditors, account numbers and approximate balances of debts, if applicable*).

14. Each Party will pay, and will be solely liable and responsible for, any debts or financial obligations solely incurred or contracted by or for him or her either before or after the date of this agreement, and each will indemnify the other against any such debts, claims or liability arising.

15. Except as otherwise expressly provided for in this document, each party hereby waives and relinquishes any claims or marital rights which each may have, now or hereinafter, under any present or future laws in the other's assets, property or estate, including but not limited to all dower and inheritance rights.

16. This Agreement shall in no way be construed as a consent to, or collusion to bring about a divorce or dissolution of marriage on the part of the parties. In the event, however, that one party (or both) sooner or later brings an action for a divorce or dissolution of marriage in a court of competent jurisdiction in a State wherein either party resides, the parties agree that the provisions of this agreement shall be binding and controlling, and be deemed the complete settlement of all marital issues between the parties and that the said provisions of this agreement shall further be incorporated, in full and in substance, into the resultant Judgment of Divorce or Dissolution, by reference. This Agreement shall not be merged into any such judgment of divorce or dissolution, but shall survive and be separately binding on the parties.

17. This Agreement shall be interpreted in accordance with the laws of the State in the United States where one or both of the parties live (i.e., is permanently domiciled) at any given time.

IN WITNESS WHEREOF, the parties hereby voluntarily sign, seal and acknowledge this agreement in duplicate originals, one of which is retained by each of the parties hereto, this____ day of ____________, 19__.

SIGNED: ______________________________ ______________________
(Husband) (Date of Signing)

Present Address: ____

____

SIGNED: ______________________________ ______________________
(Wife) (Date of Signing)

Present Address: ____

VERIFICATION

STATE OF ______________:
COUNTY OF ____________: **SS.**

On this date, the ____day of _________. 19__, before me, a Notary Public in and for the State and County captioned above, personally appeared Mr. ________________________, personally known or made known to me to be the person who executed the foregoing SEPARATION/SETTLEMENT Agreement, and the said person stated under oath under penalties of perjury, that the facts and statements contained in this document are true and that he freely and voluntarily executed the said agreement for the purposes named therein.

WITNESS my hand and seal. ______________________________
(Notary Stamp/Signature)

STATE OF ________________:
COUNTY OF ______________: SS.

On this date, the ____day of _________. 19__, before me, a Notary Public in and for the State and County captioned above, personally appeared Mr. ______________________, personally known or made known to me to be the person who executed the foregoing SEPARATION/SETTLEMENT Agreement, and the said person stated under oath under penalties of perjury, that the facts and statements contained in this document are true and that he freely and voluntarily executed the said agreement for the purposes named therein.

WITNESS my hand and seal.

____
(Notary Stamp/Signature)

CERTIFICATION BY SUBSCRIBING WITNESSES TO AGREEMENT

We, the undersigned witness(es) whose names are hereunto subscribed, DO HEREBY CERTIFY under the penalty of perjury, that on the _____________ day of ___________ 19__, both of the parties above named, respectively signed their names to this instrument in our presence and in the presence of each of us and at the same time, in our presence and to our hearing, the said persons declared the same to be their Written Agreement, made by and freely agreed to by them, and requested us and each of us, to sign our names thereto as witnesses to the execution thereof, which we hereby do in the presence of the parties and of each other, on the day of the date of the said execution. The said parties appeared to be under no duress, force, compulsion or constraint of any kind when they signed the said agreement.

SIGNED:

(1) ______________________________ of ______________________________
(Signature and Name) (Address)

(2) ______________________________ of ______________________________
(Signature and Name) (Address)

(3) ______________________________ of ______________________________
(Signature and Name) (Address)

CHAPTER 7

LET'S SIGN THE WRITTEN AGREEMENT: FOLLOW THESE PROCEDURES FOR THE ALL-IMPORTANT "EXECUTION" OF THE AGREEMENT

A. This Execution Phase Is Of The Utmost Importance

After an agreement is drawn up (the subject matter of the preceding Chapter 6), the next order of business is the "***Execution***" phase (the signing) of the document by the two principal partners. Technically speaking, *the execution phase of the making of the agreement is probably the most critical part of the whole process.* Indeed, to sum it up IN ONE WORD, SUFFICE IT SIMPLY TO SAY THIS: THE SIGNING EVENT IN THE MAKING OF THE AGREEMENT IS THE KEY ITEM, EASILY THE SINGLE MOST VITAL EVENT IN THE MAKING OF A LEGALLY VALID AGREEMENT. This is so for the simple reason that, over and above the issue of the content of the agreement, the execution act is the key piece of event the courts look to in determining whether an agreement is, indeed, the free, informed, consensual act of the parties. ***Therefore, this is an extremely important and most serious business and should be treated with the utmost care and attention to every detail by the agreement makers.***

B. Some Recommended Practical "Ceremonies" For a Valid Signing

The relevant rules of each state stipulate certain basic procedures or requirements for a valid "execution" (signing) of the agreement.* ***It's to ensure that the requirements of almost every state whatsoever are met, and to ensure the most effective "execution" of the agreement, that we suggest this: YOU (BOTH PARTIES) MUST STRICTLY FOLLOW THESE STEP-BY-STEP "CEREMONIES" OR PROCEDURES TO SIGN YOUR AGREEMENT.***

FIRST: Let's say that you and your spouse (or partner) have set a date when the signing event is to take place. Thereafter, it is highly advised that you look for at least two adult persons (one person from each party's side) who you are to invite to the signing event who are to act as witnesses to the signing*. At least one, but preferably two witnesses (one person from each party's side) will usually suffice. And they could be anybody (parents of either of the spouses, your adult children, relatives, friends, neighbors, etc.), providing they are over 18 years of age and generally of sound mind and character. *Note that it is not necessary —indeed, it is not usually advisable—that the witness (es) (or Notary Public) should read or know the specific contents of the agreement at the time of the agreement signing.* It is sufficient if the spouses should merely tell the witness(es) at the time, that the document presented before them is the couple's separation (or settlement and ante-nuptial) agreement and that the couple merely request that they bear witnesses to the signing event.

---

*In actuality, not all states require (in fact, only one or two actually do require) that the agreement be specifically signed before witnesses. However, this is highly advised herein because, as a practical matter, the use of witnesses is almost always beneficial and advisable in this type of event in that it can only enhance, not detract from, the legitimacy of the agreement before any court of law, making it much harder for one spouse or the other to come up with a claim that he or she was somehow forced into signing an agreement against his/her will, or that he/she did it under less than normal conditions. An important prerequisite in proving the validity of an agreement of this sort between marital parties, is evidence that the parties dealt at an "arm's length" with each other — i.e., genuine, business like, bonafide dealings that were neither 'forced' nor rushed or based on obviously unreasonable terms.

Get a colored ink pen ready, also, to be taken to the signing event for use in signing the agreement.

SECOND: O.K. Let's assume that you and your spouse (or partner) have now gathered at the designated place for the signing affair, along with the invited witnesses. You and your spouse (or partner) should excuse yourselves from the rest in the house and get into a separate room to privately read the agreement.

Using *three* copies of the final draft of the agreement you prepared, each spouse should read out the contents of the agreement to the other, going clause by clause, and asking questions of each other to make sure the provisions are fully understood and taken note of by both parties.

THIRD: Next, you both should then rejoin your witnesses, if any, after you shall have both finished reading the contents to each other. Briefly inform the witnesses present of the following:

I) that the document you and your spouse have in front of you, about to sign, is an agreement of separation with each other (or a settlement or living-together or premarital agreement, as the case may be); 2) that both of you have just fully read the contents and are about to sign this agreement with full comprehension of the provisions and with free and voluntary consent to its provisions; and 3) that you invite them to sign their own names after you as witnesses to the signing.

(You may say something like: ***"Gentlemen and/or ladies), this document is our separation and Settlement Agreement [or, living-together agreement, or premarital agreement, as the case may be]. Both of us, Mary and John, have read it, and completely comprehend the provisions and implications. We freely and voluntarily consent to its provisions, and ask you to witness our signatures, and to sign your names after us as witnesses".*** If this statement is made by one spouse (or partner), at the end of the statement the speaking spouse, say the Husband, will add: ***"And Mary, just for the record, is everything just said correct and true?" Mary: "YES!"***

FOURTH: With that statement made (and the other spouse's response), as the witnesses attentively watch you, <u>each</u> spouse should take turn to sign. One party will, first, initial and date each and every page of the agreement (just the three originals) at the bottom left-hand margin space, and then sign it on the last page where the agreement ends, in the appropriate space provided for "Husband" or "Wife." SIGN IN COLORED INK ONLY. (This way, the original document could be differentiated.) Then, print your name just below your signature (at the end of the agreement). Fill in the date of the signing at the last page. Then, the other spouse or party will do exactly the same. [Each party should examine the documents and counter check to be sure that all three copies are initialed, dated and signed by <u>both</u> parties in each spot required].

FIFTH: It will now be the turn of the witnesses to sign. Ask each of the witnesses to read the paragraph just following the last page of the Agreement under the caption **"Certification By Witnesses"** — the one just coming after or below your own signatures. (Note that it is not necessary that the contents of the agreement be read by or made known to the witnesses; in fact, it is advised against!)

Then, as you watch each of the witnesses, they would take turns to sign and enter their individual addresses in the spaces provided for them. Only after that — after all of the witnesses have signed their own names--should anybody in the group leave the room, or be joined by anyone else not in the signing group. [The role of the witnesses is over, and they may now leave if they wish].

NOTE: The central point of engaging in the formalities ("ceremonies") of Agreement-signing should be clearly borne in mind. The idea is to make the event MEMORABLE to those who participated, especially to the witnesses — to make the event "stick out" in their minds, so that they'll always recall the event, however remotely or vaguely, if or when it should ever become necessary that they be called upon to do so.

SIXTH: In all you do, whether in the negotiations or in the actual signing of the agreement, avoid the appearance of haste or hush. Even though you and your spouse may have been in accord on all the terms of the agreement, don't sign the documents hurriedly after the start of negotiations. Events have to appear as though everybody has been given every opportunity and an ample time for thinking things over.

SEVENTH: YOU AND YOUR SPOUSE OR PARTNER SHOULD NOW HAVE THE AGREEMENT NOTARIZED. There's one more important thing you should do before you're done. You and your spouse (or partner) should take the Agreement (all three originals) with you and have them notarized in the presence of a Notary public. Under the laws of most states, for the purpose of using the agreement as a "stipulation" or "petition" in a future divorce or other court action, it is required that the agreements be "acknowledged" before a Notary Public.

It's simple! Simply take the document (both parties) to a Notary Public and there, have the agreements and your own signatures "notarized" and "acknowledged" by the notary. (Ordinarily, under most states rules, except when title to real property is involved, an agreement which is not notarized or acknowledged, however, does not necessarily become invalid just on account of that. It will still remain legally valid, in such an instance. Nevertheless, it does add to the strength of the agreement to always have it notarized, regardless.)

EIGHTH: ***What To Do With The Finished Signed Agreements.*** What do you do with the signed and completed agreements? Simply, the wife (or one partner) keeps a copy, and the husband (or the other partner) keeps one. And what do you do with the third copy? This you will have to file with the County clerk's office of your county of residence (or your spouse's) in the state wherein the agreement is made, if a formal court filing is required under your state's procedures.

C. Filing of the Agreement With the County Clerk's Office May be Required in Certain States

Under the laws of certain states, upon completion of a separation or property settlement agreement, a true copy of the agreement, — or a Memorandum of that agreement — is required to be promptly filed with the County Clerk's office (or a recorder of deed's office). Such public filing or recordation is not generally required for a cohabitation or premarital type of agreement, however. New York is one state which has this filing requirement. North Carolina and some other states also requires filing of the agreement. *The overwhelming majority of states do not require a court filing of the agreement, however.* Parties in other states may ascertain whether filing is required in their states by simply calling the office of their local county court's clerk in charge of matrimonial and domestic relations. (See Appendix C for the name of the appropriate matrimonial court to call for your state.)

Under New York State's rules, for example, the procedures of filing are simple. You'll merely submit the Memorandum of Agreement (see sample of the form on p. 66) to the office of the County Clerk of the State Supreme Court in the specific county in which either you or your spouse lives. (There's a filing fee charged for this — $170 in New York as of this writing). The court clerk will assign you an "index number" which you will then affix to the Memorandum Form and then have it filed away with the clerk, along with a copy of the agreement. Now, make sure you also enter this number on your own respective copies of the Separation Agreement as this is the court's official identifying number by which your case could be traced at any time in the future. NOW IT IS FINALLY DONE!

D. Some Few Final Words On Post-Agreement Matters

Your Separation (or Settlement) agreement is now concluded. You may now go home and rest assured. But while you do that, it would be helpful to **have a few more final facts in mind as you put your separation document away:**

FIRST: You must bear in mind that if there is a reconciliation or an extended period of living together between you and your spouse after you have both signed the agreement and physically lived apart from each other, the separation may be deemed automatically revoked from the date of such a reconciliation or living together. (So the law says!)

SECOND: Bear in mind that in most states, especially in the so-called "no-fault" divorce states, after a certain period of time has passed from the date of your entering into the agreement or the physical separation,* either of the spouses *may*, if so inclined, use the agreement itself as a ground or "cause" for bringing an action for a divorce — providing, however, that: 1) you did not reconcile or resume living together at any time after the signing of the agreement; and 2) that the spouse who is bringing the divorce action (the "plaintiff"), did comply with his/her own obligations under the agreement.

THIRD: Remember that, for most practical purposes, a separation agreement is more or less the same thing as a property settlement agreement. Hence, the terms of either kind of agreement, when available, would generally and gladly be acceptable to just about every divorce court in settling the disposition of a couple's property, their maintenance, and the support, custody and visitation of their children, and the like.

---

* **The minimum length of time a couple must live apart before they may use the fact of a separation as a cause of action for a divorce differs from state to state. In general, however, it averages between 1 and 2 years; in New York State, it's one year (or more) from the date of signing.**

Sample I

MEMORANDUM OF AGREEMENT OF SETTLEMENT/SEPARATION (New York Version)

(a) The names and addresses of each of the parties:

Husband: ____

Wife: ____

(b) The parties were married at: ____________________, On this date: __________
(City and State)

(c) Time Agreement of Separation was made (signed) on this date: ______________

(d) The date of the subscription and acknowledgment of such Agreement of Separation

Date of Notary, is: ____________________

Dated: ____________________

Signed: ____________________
(Husband)

Name (Print) ____________________

Signed: ____________________
(Wife)

Name (Print) ____________________

State of ____________________

County of ____________________ SS.:

On the ______ day of ________ 19__, before me came Mr/Mrs ______________________,

to me known or made known to me to be the individual described in, and who executed, the foregoing instrument, and acknowledged to me that he executed the same.

(NOTARY PUBLIC)

State of ____________________

County of ____________________ SS.:

On the ______ day of ________ 19__, before me came Mr/Mrs ______________________,

to me known or made known to me to be the individual described in, and who executed, the foregoing instrument, and acknowledged to me that _he executed the same

(NOTARY PUBLIC)

<u>**Sample 2**</u>

Memorandum of Separation/Settlement Agreement - For Use In Making Public Recordation Of Agreement (North Carolina Version)

The State of ______________________
County of _____________________ s.s.:

MEMORANDUM OF SEPARATION AGREEMENT

THIS MEMORANDUM OF SEPARATION AGREEMENT made and entered into this _____ day of _____________, 19__, by and between _________________, hereinafter referred to as "HUSBAND", and ________________, hereinafter referred to as "WIFE", both of ______________ County, State of ___________.

WITNESSETH:

WHEREAS, the above-named Husband and Wife do hereby certify unto whom it may concern that on __________, 19__, they entered into a Separation Agreement and Property Settlement which is now in effect and contains provisions allowing Husband and Wife to live separate and apart and to deal with their properties and estates as if unmarried.

NOW, THEREFORE, pursuant to the laws of the state of ___________, the parties do hereby execute this Memorandum of Separation Agreement for the purposes of public recordation and announcement of the agreement, by setting forth the following:

1. *Separation.* It is agreed that the parties hereto separated on _______________, 19__, with the intent to live separate and apart from each other as from and after such date, and that from and after such date, Husband and Wife have and shall continue to live separate and apart, each free from the marital control and authority of the other to the same extent as though each were single and unmarried. Each of the parties shall have the right to reside at such place or places and with such person or persons as she or he may desire or deem fit, and to conduct, carry on and engage in any employment, business, trade or profession he or she may desire, choose, or deem fit, the same to be for his or her own separate use and benefit, and free from any and all control, restraint, interference, directly or indirectly, on the part of the other.

2. *Mutual Release.* The Husband and Wife do hereby waive, release, discharge, quitclaim and renounce each to the other, and to their respective heirs and assigns, all rights to claim an equal or equitable distribution of property or distributive award pursuant to the inheritance laws of this or any other state, all rights to a share in the estate upon the death of the other, all rights to elect to take a life estate upon the death of the other, all rights to a year's allowance upon the death of the other, all rights to take under or dissent from the will of the other, all rights to act as administrator or executor of the other's estate, and any and all other rights which either party may now have, or hereafter acquire against the other under the present or future laws of any jurisdiction arising out of the marital relationship.

Each party releases and discharges the other from all causes of action, claims, rights, or demands in law or equity, which either party may now have, or may hereafter acquire against the other under the present or future laws of any jurisdiction, except any and all causes of action for divorce, based on any legal ground for divorce that might exist in any jurisdiction in which either party may become a resident. The Husband and Wife grant, release and forever quitclaim each to the other all right, title, interest, claim and demand whatsoever in the real property which the other now owns or may hereafter acquire, and each party may hereafter purchase, acquire, own, hold, posses, encumber, dispose of and convey any and all classes and kinds of real and personal property as though unmarried, free from the consent, joinder, and interference of the other party.

3. *Representation to Purchasers.* It is agreed that all persons dealing with the Husband and Wife hereafter may rely upon this *Memorandum of Separation Agreement* as containing all the provisions for the Separation Agreement material to the said parties being authorized to acquire, hold, manage, transfer and convey their real property and estate without the knowledge or consent of joinder of their spouse.

4, *Additional Instruments.* Each of the parties shall from time to time at the request of the other, execute, acknowledge and deliver to the other party all further instruments that may be reasonably required to give full force and effect to the provisions of this agreement.

IN TESTIMONY WHEREOF, the parties have set their hands and seals to this Memorandum of Separation Agreement in duplicate, one copy of which is retained by each of the parties the day and year first above written.

Signed: ______________________________
(Husband)

Signed: ______________________________
(Wife)

State of: ______________________________

County of: ____________ S.S.:

I, ____________________, a Notary Public in and for above-designated County and State, do hereby certify that ____________________, and ____________________, personally appeared before me this day and that they acknowledged the due execution of the foregoing separation agreement and property settlement.

WITNESS my hand and notarial seal this _________ day of ____________, 19__.

____
(Notary Public)

CHAPTER 8

EVERY QUESTION YOU MAY WANT ANSWERED ABOUT HETEROSEXUAL/HOMOSEXUAL COHABITATION, THE "MARVIN CASE," AND PROPERTY RIGHTS OF NON-MARITAL COUPLES

A. WHAT IS THE PRESENT STATE OF THE LAW IN REGARD TO NON-MARITAL COHABITATION?

By and large, the law governing relations between unmarried or non-marital ("cohabiting") partners still remains an uncharted legal jungle in which anything may still turn out one way or the other. For the most part, it is yet a murky legal — or even social — area to be fully developed in the years ahead. True, it is still rare to find any state which has enacted any specific laws in this area. However, the courts of many states, notably those of California, Washington, New York and others, have taken it upon themselves to hand down some decisions concerning such relationships, especially with respect to the division or allocation of property. In deed, it is rare to find a knowledgeable legal expert or observer in the matrimonial relations scene who does not now predict that the famous California (Marvin) decision, the pioneering decision in the nation on the matter, is a legal "precedent" soon to be duplicated in the rest of the country.

There has been, in recent times, a dramatic and still growing increase in the number of adult Americans who simply choose to cohabit with each other without the benefit of a marriage. And the same thing has also been true of the number of marriage-age young Americans who have either never married at all, or have not bothered to marry after being divorced.* ***All in all, the growing significance of this area in family law courtrooms, make it necessary that persons involved in any sort of living-together arrangements be familiar with some basics on this.***

B. ANSWERS TO EVERYTHING YOU PROBABLY WANT TO KNOW ON COHABITATION LAW

What follows, in question and answer format, may answer some of the questions that have, so far, been answered by the courts in the so-called "cohabitation law issues," especially by the nationally influential state courts of California, Washington State, New Jersey and New York, among others.

QUESTION 1: Is cohabitation legally permissible in every state?

ANSWER: No. Many states have laws prohibiting persons of opposite sex (or the same sex) from living together without being married with various penalties attached for violation of that rule. It is basically a carry over from the

---

* According to a U.S. Census Bureau report released in April 1978, the number of Americans, most of whom were under the age of 25, who were cohabiting in March of 1977 was 1,508,000, up 14% from the 1976 level, and over 130% from 1970: the proportion of all women aged 20-24 who had never been married, rose from 28% in 1960 to 45% in 1977, and from 53% to 64% for men during the same period. The number of divorces from 1970-1977 increased 79% with 8 million divorced persons choosing not to remarry. Overall, the number of couples who were living together without being married in 1974 was about 8 times what it was 10 years earlier. It should be pointed out, though that although the number of nonmarital-couple households has more than doubled since 1970, such households still make up only 3 percent of all couples living together in the United States.

common law where open and notorious sexual conduct outside of marriage was deemed offensive by and to the public.

As of this writing, some laws against non-marital cohabitation still exist in the following states: Arizona, Florida, Idaho, Illinois, Michigan, Mississippi, New Mexico, North Carolina, North Dakota, Virginia, and West Virginia.

To be sure, as a practical matter these laws are rarely enforced though sometimes they are.

QUESTION 2: What about living together among gay or lesbian couples? Are there any states in which this is recognized as a legal marital relationship of some kind?

ANSWER. To our knowledge, no state has yet accorded legal validity or recognition (by way, that is, of enacted statute) to gay/lesbian couples' relationships. While "cohabitation" between unmarried persons of opposite sex is still not exactly viewed with favor in much of the country, cohabitation relationships among persons of the same sex are by and large viewed as immoral, sinful and illegal in virtually every state, subject to state sanctions of varying degrees. However, all indications are that such state of affairs notwithstanding, in practice the practice of living together by gay and lesbian couples is widely tolerated by the authorities in most states, and that an otherwise valid property settlement agreement, even among homosexual couples, would enjoy the same kind of recognition and legality generally accorded non-marital agreements, as outlined below elsewhere in this chapter.

QUESTION 3 where do we stand with the law, today, on homosexuality and sodomy?

ANSWER: As of this writing in 1994, it is safe to say that in many states, though by no means all, homosexuality per se still remains strictly against the law. And so is the homosexual act of sodomy — defined by law as "any sex act involving the sex organs of one person and the mouth or anus of another."

The landmark ruling on the matter to date, is the 5-4 decision by the U.S. Supreme Court in June 1986, involving a sodomy charge against Michael Hardwick, an Atlanta Georgia man.

Hardwick had been observed by a police office performing oral sex on another man. A Federal district judge initially dismissed the case on procedural grounds, but a three-judge panel of the United States Court of Appeals subsequently ruled in May 1985 that the Georgia anti-sodomy law was unconstitutional in that it unduly interfered with "certain individual decisions critical to personal autonomy because those decisions are essentially private."

The state of Georgia appealed arguing that sodomy is an unnatural act and a crime against the laws of God and man. The Supreme Court, in its decision, ruled that the constitution does not protect homosexual relations between consenting adults even in the privacy of their own homes and that the Georgia law could be used to prosecute homosexual and other persons who engage in oral and anal sex. Writing for the Court, Justice Byron White rejected the view "that any kind of private sexual conduct between consenting adults is constitutionally insulated from state proscription." Quite to the contrary, he stated, the Federal Constitution does not "confer a fundamental right upon homosexuals to engage in sodomy and hence [does not] invalidate the laws of many states that still make such conduct illegal and have done so for a very long time." In short, any state, if it chooses, may prohibit the act of homosexuality, and it would presumably be within its constitutional sphere of authority to do so.

Today, there are twenty-six states that have decriminalized sodomy, and five of the twenty-four that still make homosexual sodomy a crime have decriminalized heterosexual sodomy at least in some contexts.

The following are the states without a sodomy law: Alaska, California, Colorado, Connecticut, Delaware, Hawaii, Illinois, Indiana, Iowa, Maine, Massachusetts, Nebraska, New Hampshire, New Jersey, New Mexico, New York, North Dakota, Ohio, Oregon, Pennsylvania, South Dakota, Vermont, Washington, West Virginia, Wisconsin, and Wyoming.

The following are the states that have heterosexual and homosexual sodomy laws: Alabama, Arizona, Florida, Georgia, Idaho, Kentucky, Louisiana, Maryland, Michigan, Minnesota, Mississippi, Missouri, North Carolina, Oklahoma, Rhode Island, South Carolina, Tennessee, Utah, Virginia, and Washington, D.C.

States with a homosexual sodomy law only are: Arkansas, Kansas, Montana, Nevada, and Texas.

Many cities and communities across the country, however, have attempted to balance the scales somewhat by passing homosexual rights laws. In New York City, for example, the city council, after rejecting a homosexual rights bill for fifteen years, finally enacted Local Law 2 on March 20, 1986, banning discrimination on the basis of sexual orientation in housing, employment, and public accommodations.

QUESTION 4: In a state where, as is frequently the case, the legislature has not enacted any laws to govern the distribution of property acquired by cohabiting persons during their relationship, by what "law" would the courts go in deciding a property settlement dispute between such persons?

ANSWER: The courts would rely solely on their "judicial judgment" in deciding such cases, since there's no body of statutes to go by.

QUESTION 5: Are there any general principles which the courts would employ in deciding such cases?

ANSWER: Yes, in the famous "Marvin case" of California, the California Supreme Court, a leader in matrimonial law innovation, seemed to have set forth another precedent which many other states have to varying degrees copied on this question. In that case, decided in 1976, the California high court laid down the following rules as "the principles which should govern distribution of property acquired in a non-marital relationship":

"1) The courts should enforce express contracts between non-marital partners except to the extent that the contract is explicitly founded on the consideration of meretricious sexual services; and 2) in the absence of an **express contract ****, the courts should inquire into the conduct of the parties to determine whether that conduct demonstrates an **implied contract****, agreement of partnership or joint venture, or some other tacit understanding between the parties. The courts may also employ the doctrine of **quantum meruit****, or equitable remedies such as **constructive or resulting trusts****, when warranted by the facts of the case."

QUESTION 6: What does this really mean in simple layman's language?

ANSWER: These are what the California court is saying:

i.) that persons who are just cohabiting or having sexual relations but are not married to each other, have just as much legal right to enter into a lawful contract as any other persons, just like persons who are either married to each other, or are unmarried to any one, in ordinary contractual business relations.

ii.) that where there's any contract between two (or more) non-marital partners that is of "express" (i.e. spoken or written) type, the courts would enforce the provisions of that express contract *except* those provisions that are "explicitly founded on the consideration of meretricious sexual services" — that is, those provisions which ***explicitly***

** See Glossary of Legal Terms (Appendix B) for definition.

say, in effect, 'I owe or give you this or that property or income, in return for your owing or giving me your sexual services'.

iii.) that where, on the other hand, there's ***no*** "express" contract between the non-marital partners, in such a situation, says the California high court, the courts would enforce any apparent understanding or "implied contract" between the parties — that is, any understanding the courts can infer or "imply" from the conducts or circumstances of the parties as indicative of what they meant to do, if any.

iv.) that, depending on the facts of a particular case, the Court may, among other remedies, allocate the property of the parties to one or the other partner on the following basis: a) on the principle of "according to what he or she deserves" (the legal doctrine of quantum meruit); or b) the Court could use its "independent judicial judgment" to determine that one or the other partner should really have been entitled to a certain property, even though it may not have been so expressly stated by the parties, or even if the property may have been held in "trust" in the other partner's name ("constructive" or "resulting" trust).

QUESTION 7: What is a "meretricious sexual" service or consideration?

ANSWER: Basically, this is an explicit pledge or promise of a sexual service by one unmarried person to another (or between two persons who are not married to each other), as a condition for entering into a relationship or for doing or getting something. The reason that such a conduct is "meretricious", is because it is immoral and illicit, by society's standards, and against the generally accepted "public policy" of promoting the institution of marriage.

For example, if a woman *expressly* says to a man to whom she is not married: 'Let's make an agreement. I'll just live with you as your wife and bear you children.' And the man says, 'O.K. And I'll provide for you and give you my home.' This is a contract or understanding that is based on "meretricious" (i.e., immoral and illicit) consideration, because the woman is offering adultery, or, at least, fornication, prostitution and illegitimacy, in return for the man's material support. Another example might be where a contract requires that one or both parties would divorce their spouses, or rewards them for doing so, since it's considered to be in the public policy that marriage and the stability of the institution be promoted, not undermined.

QUESTION 8: Since it is still generally considered illicit and immoral (or, at least, not the model behavior) for persons who are not married to each other to live together and engage in sexual relations, does the mere living together by such persons automatically disqualify an agreement between them or automatically make it unlawful?

ANSWER: No. The courts have ruled that while such a relationship may be immoral alright, it does not, in and of itself, disqualify the partners from entering into a lawful agreement with each other. It does not make an agreement between them automatically unlawful, *as long as the (immoral) relationship itself was not made a consideration of their agreement* — i.e., so long as the immoral relationship was not the thing that was promised or pledged to induce either of them to enter into the agreement. Where, for example, the conveyance or transfer of a property from one non-marital partner to another was not made for the purpose of inducing or prolonging illicit cohabitation, a resulting trust or agreement between the parties involved in the illicit cohabitation does not necessarily become automatically illegal.

QUESTION 9: What if only some parts of a contract, but not the whole contract, made between cohabiting partners is "explicitly founded upon immoral and illicit consideration of meretricious sexual services", does that mean that the entire contract is doomed?

ANSWER: No. In all cases, the court is required to examine each contract on a case-by-case basis, and if it can determine that there is a "separable" portion of a contract which was not based on a meretricious sexual consideration, it would separate out that portion and enforce that portion *only*.

QUESTION 10: What is the courts' attitude towards the property rights of partners who are involved in a putative marriage or relationship?

ANSWER: In general, property acquired during such a relationship is considered as "quasi-marital" property, and may therefore be divided between the partners in accord with the same laws governing division of property in regular dissolution of marriages. In California, for example the courts have ruled that putative spouses may recover for the reasonable value of the service they rendered to the putative household, less the value of the support they had received up until the time of the discovery of the invalidity of the marriage. It has also been ruled that both the "guilty" spouse (i.e., the one who was aware all along that the marriage was not valid), and the "innocent" spouse (i.e., the one who was not), are entitled to one-half of the property acquired during the relationship under the California Community property rule.

QUESTION 11: What if I had merely promised my non-marital partner that I would perform homemaking service for him and went ahead and did just that , is that a lawful and sufficient "consideration" for a contract?

ANSWER: Yes, nowadays it is. You don't have to pay back in money. Your household services are just as valuable.

QUESTION 12: What sort of things or factors do the courts look for to determine whether or not a non-marital relationship qualifies for property division or compensation rights under the principles we've been discussing?

ANSWER: They include factors like one or more of the following:
Did the parties live together, especially for several years (in a stable, long-term relationship), rather than just being engaged in a casual relationship from time to time; and did they "hold themselves out" to friends, associates or relatives as husband and wife — in terms, for example, of say rearing children together, purchasing a home or other property together, obtaining credit or maintaining bank accounts jointly, filing joint income tax returns, introducing each other as a "husband" or "wife" to the public, or otherwise conducting themselves as if they were married?

Did the parties have an agreement or a reasonable understanding of some sort (oral or written or implied) to live together and combine or pull their efforts, earnings, or assets; or, was there a reasonable expectation or understanding by one or both of them that each would share in any property accumulated by the parties?

Did each of the parties contribute some service or income to the relationship (e.g., as a companion, caretaker of the house or children, homemaker, cook or provider for the household, etc.)? Did one (or both) of the parties give up or sacrifice something of value just on account of the non-marital relationship, or because of an understanding or arrangement made because of the relationship (e.g., giving up a career, especially if it can be shown that it was a promising or flourishing one before the party was compelled to abandon it in order to devote time to the non-marital relationship)?

Is there a reasonable indication (either written, oral, or implied from the conduct of the parties) that one or both of the parties reasonably expected to be provided for or to be supported financially by the other?

In general, the test is whether the general relationship between the parties and the way they conducted themselves towards each other reasonably indicate an intention to establish a long-term relationship and joint activities — the sort of relationship that is ordinarily associated with "married" couples.

QUESTION 13: If the parties in a non-marital relationship had lived together for a long time but still did not take that final step of getting married, wouldn't the Court interpret that as a strong indication that they never planned or intended to share their earnings or property, in the first place?

ANSWER: Not necessarily. The rule established by the California Supreme Court in the Marvin case, is that it is unwise to jump to the assumption or conclusion that the parties intended to keep their earnings and property separate and independent merely because they lived together for a long time and did not get married. The court said that "the parties' intention can only be ascertained by more searching inquiry (by the courts) into the nature of their relationship." That:

> Some non-marital couples may wish to avoid the permanent commitment that marriage implies, but still be willing to share any property acquired during their relationship.
> Some may not want to get married because they entertain some fears of losing a pension, welfare or tax benefits, etc.
> Some may engage in a non-marital relationship as a "test period" before deciding on getting married.
> Some may just not be able, at the moment, to afford the difficulties or expenses involved in getting a former marriage dissolved to allow for a remarriage.
> Some may believe (correctly or incorrectly) that a common-law marriage is valid in the particular state.

QUESTION 14: You hear so much about the "Marvin Case" lately. What was the case all about?

ANSWER: This was, in a word, the famous "landmark" California case that has just about revolutionized all the traditional concepts and practices in the country regarding cohabitation between unmarried persons.

Michelle Marvin (she had changed her last name legally from Triola to Marvin just before her relationship with Mr. Marvin ended), had lived for nearly 7 years with Lee Marvin, an Academy award-winning actor, without being married to him—from October 1964 through May 1970. During this period, a lot of property was acquired, including real estate, personal property and motion picture rights said to be worth over $3 million, but all were in Mr. Marvin's name. Then in May 1970, Mr. Marvin asked Ms. Marvin to move out of the couple's household. Mr. Marvin continued to support her, though, until November 1971 when he stopped doing so. Ms. Marvin sued Mr. Marvin to court. In court, Ms. Marvin claimed that the couple had made an oral "contract" under which she was to get one-half of all the property accumulated by the couple during their relationship, as well as support for life in return for her companionship; and that she had given up a singing career on the strength of this promise just to serve as his cook, companion and confidante.

The lower court (the Superior Court) denied Ms. Marvin's suit, on the ground that such a contract between two unmarried persons was an agreement for prostitution. The decision against Ms. Marvin was further upheld on an appeal. Again, however, Ms. Marvin appealed to the Supreme Court of California. And, in its decision, handed down on December 27, 1976, the State's Supreme Court reversed the decision of the two lower courts. The court then went ahead and set down some general "principles" which it said should govern judicial decisions in all future similar cases. It then ordered the Marvin case sent back to the original (superior) court for a new trial.

Thus, a new precedent with potentially far and wide implications, was set for deciding disputes involving property rights among persons engaged in cohabitation situations.

QUESTION 15: What happened when the Marvin case was retried in the lower court?

ANSWER: The case was retried before Judge Arthur Marshall of the Los Angeles Superior Court. And in its new decision in April of 1979, the court said it found no basis or proof that Ms. Marvin had either an "express" or "implicit" contract with Mr. Marvin calling for the two to share Mr. Marvin's assets and earnings (which was now estimated to be $3.6 million.) Therefore, said the court, Ms. Marvin was not entitled to share the Marvin assets because to authorize that " would mean that the court would recognize each unmarried person living together to be automatically entitled by such living together and performing spouse-like functions to half of the property bought with the earnings of the other non-marital partner." This would in effect mean, Judge Marshall said, recognizing the concept of common-law marriages which had been abolished by law in California since 1895.

QUESTION 16: But wasn't Ms. Marvin awarded some money by Judge Marshall?

ANSWER: Yes, she was. She was awarded only $104,000 (not the one-half of $3.6 million she sought). **But, more important, look at the reason on which the Judge based the award. It was made only for reasons of "rehabilitation purposes"— the so-called "rehabilitative alimony".** In other words, the reason that any money at all was awarded to Ms. Marvin in this case, was *not* because the court agreed that she had any contract with Mr. Marvin which entitled her to compensation for her live-in time, but because the court felt that it was only fair that she be given something— "so that she may have the economic means to re-educate herself and to learn new employable skills." *

On a subsequent appeal of the amount of the award by Ms. Marvin, however, the California Court of Appeal ruled in August 1981 that not even the $104,000 award to her ought to be paid to Ms. Marvin, "since the award itself is without support in either equity or law." This ruling stood and became the final word on the case to date when, in October 1981, the California Supreme Court — the State's highest — refused to review the Court of Appeal's decision.

QUESTION 17: What, in the final analysis, could be said to be the ultimate message and significance that came out of this whole famous, landmark Marvin case in the field of matrimonial law in America?

ANSWER: The fundamental, lasting significance about the Marvin decision was that it was a step in the direction of giving legal protection to cohabiting parties who do not have the benefit of marriage. The court's decision was that if in its determination Marvin and Triola had, in fact, had an agreement, it would have been enforceable. *Hence, growing out of the Marvin case, it became clear that if you are an unmarried partner and want the court to give you some of the same rights to which a married person is entitled, you had better be sure to meet certain criteria; more particularly, you had better be able to show that there is some kind of contractual obligation on the part of your partner to give you what you are asking for.*

Thus, if for example, you seek support from your partner and you are unmarried to him (or her), you had better be prepared to establish that that demand is based on some kind of a contractual agreement made between the two of you. In essence, in the absence of a written agreement or some proof of an oral agreement, the unmarried man or woman who makes some kind of financial claim on his partner would likely wind up getting nothing! So, you can begin to see why many lawyers knowledgeable in the field generally advise on the need for a written agreement by cohabiting non-marital partners.

QUESTION 18: What are the various kinds of financial arrangements which non-marital partners may lawfully consider or make, by contract or otherwise?

ANSWER: They vary from case to case, depending on a couples' preference. However, here are some of the forms the arrangements might take:

> Parties may choose to keep their separate earnings and property separate, but agree to compensate one party for service which benefits the other.
> They may choose to pool only a part of their earnings and property together.
> They may choose to form a partnership or joint venture.
> They may choose to hold any property acquired in the relationship as "joint tenants" or as "tenants in common".

---

* Note the further implication of this decision. This new concept of "rehabilitative alimony" implies, perhaps for the first time, that even where there's no legal or contractual basis to award alimony or property settlement to a live-along partner, the court may, on occasion at least, still find reason or legal justification (such as the legal practice of "equitable remedy") to make an award for the "rehabilitation" needs of one or the other partner.

QUESTION 19: Some states, including California, do not recognize or permit common law marriages. Doesn't these recent Marvin-case-type decisions in California, Washington, and other states on property rights for non-marital partners really amount to a recognition of such marriages?

ANSWER: No. In the Marvin case, for example, the court made it clear that in accordance with the California statute abolishing common law marriages, it's decision was not intended to legalize common law marriages. Persons involved in such relationships would still not be entitled to the rights and privileges (e.g., inheritance rights or the widow's share of Social Security) ordinarily enjoyed by valid or even putative spouses. "We held only that she (a non-marital partner)

has the same rights to enforce contracts and to assert her equitable interest in property acquired through her effort as does any other unmarried person," the court said.

QUESTION 20: Which other states, beside California, have had similar cases involving partners who were not legally married to each other?

ANSWER: Quite a few states. One 1979 report put the number of such states then at 15, among which were the states of Washington, New Jersey, New York, Connecticut, Illinois and Oregon. And a more recent report in May 1981 put the number of states at 28, indicating the ever increasing trend.

QUESTION 21: What legal principles, if any, were established in the New Jersey case as governing non-marital cohabitants?

ANSWER: Basically, the governing principle handed down by the New Jersey Supreme Court is that promises made between two (or more) adults living together, whether married to each other or not, can constitute a legal and binding contract between the parties. This principle was laid down in the Koslowski case decided upon in June 1979.

In that case, Ms. Irma Koslowski, who had lived with Mr. Thaddeus Koslowski for 15 years without marriage, had sued Mr. Koslowski for compensation, claiming that she went to live with him because he made a verbal promise to support her for the rest of her life. The court emphasized that it was not reviving the concept of common-law marriage which had been abolished in New Jersey since 1939. However, the court added, the evidence showed that Mr. Koslowski had lured the woman away from her former husband in 1962, and had again persuaded her to return to him in 1968 when she left him after a quarrel, by promising to support her forever. That, the court said, was a valid contract.* The court awarded Ms. Koslowski a compensation of $55,000 to be paid by the man.

QUESTION 22: How about New York--what legal principles, if any, were established as governing non-marital cohabitants?

ANSWER: Basically, the governing principle handed down by New York's Court of Appeals is that a woman living with a man to whom she is not married (or a man living with a woman to whom he is not married) may be entitled to a share of his assets — providing she can prove three basic things: 1) that the parties had an "express" oral or written agreement to that effect; 2) that the complaining partner had a continuing relationship with the other partner; and 3) that the complaining partner contributed measurably to the domestic and business lives of the couple.

This principle was laid down in the Morone case decided upon in June 1980. In that case, Ms. Frances Morone, who had lived with Mr. Frank Morone for 25 years without marriage, had sued Mr. Morone for compensation, claiming that she had an (unwritten) agreement for her to provide domestic service to the man in exchange for his financial support of her and their two children. The court reasoned as follows: "(that) the difficulties attendant upon establishing property and financial rights between unmarried couples under available theories of law other than contract warrant application of

---

* The key paragraph of the New Jersey ruling, which had a somewhat close counterpart to the California ruling, is this: "We do no more than to recognize that society's mores have changed and that an agreement between adult parties living together is enforceable to the extent that it is not based on a relationship proscribed by law, or on a promise to marry."

the recognition of express contract even through the services rendered be limited to those generally characterized as 'housewifely'." Hence, the court ruled, Ms. Morone would be entitled to receive payment from her live-in companion only if she could prove to a judge or jury that there was such an "express" agreement to share in Mr. Morone's assets or earnings.

QUESTION 23: I heard that unmarried persons who live together automatically have a legal marriage after they have lived together for some period of time, say 7 years. Is this correct?

ANSWER: No. That's the "common-law marriage" myth to which there's no truth or validity whatsoever. Quite to
the contrary, what is true is that the length of a living together relationship has nothing whatsoever to do with making that relationship a legal marriage. There are only about 16 states (plus the District of Columbia) where common-law marriages are recognized as a valid marriage. Now, unless a couple lives in one of these states — and conducts itself totally in the usual husband-and-wife tradition — a living together relationship may not be recognized as a valid marital relationship, no matter how long the parties lived together.

QUESTION 24: Are there any disadvantages in having a common-law marriage rather than a legal marriage?

ANSWER: Yes. If you move out of a common-law marriage state, you automatically become unmarried, and if you move from a state which prohibits it to one which recognizes it, you'll find yourself automatically married, whether or not you want to be. Furthermore, with a common-law marriage, it may be harder to prove that a marriage existed — e.g., when you want to claim a widow's (or widower's) share of Social Security, Workman's Compensation, inheritance or alimony.

CHAPTER 9

TAX CONSIDERATIONS IN SEPARATION AND PROPERTY SETTLEMENT AGREEMENTS

A. Some Realities About Tax Consequences In Marital Agreements

Income tax implications of provisions made in separation and settlement agreements (the same as in divorce decrees) could be very important to the contracting persons. The whole subject matter, itself, is one which, because of its sheer complexity and ever-changing nature, would take a separate volume of its own to treat, and is in fact a subject often better handled by tax accountants than by lawyers. However, there's one cheerful note concerning this matter for users of this manual, namely: *for the vast majority of couples who would be involved in divorce or matrimonial settlement agreements, no significant "tax consequence" would probably ever arise*, anyway. *Except for the category of relatively few couples who are fortunate enough to fall under the upper echelons of the society's income earners or property owners, significant knowledge of tax laws and record-keeping would not be necessary.**

Nevertheless, it would be useful for you to be aware of a few main tips and pointers on taxes for divorced or separated persons. There's some truth in the statement of one New York city matrimonial lawyer that, "no (matrimonial) agreement may be intelligently arrived at without consideration of the tax impact." This may be true in light of the fact that, nowadays, most settlement agreements wind up being used as a framework on which divorce terms are eventually based. We highlight below, therefore, a few (and only a few) significant general principles of income taxation normally applicable in divorce and legal separation cases.

B. Some Major Critical Tax Considerations

The Tax Reform Act of 1984 [P.L. 98-369, 98th Cong. ζ422 (a), (b)] made sweeping changes in the tax laws relating to domestic relations. And in that context, among the major critical tax considerations that are important, are the following:

1) Whether alimony payments will be deductible by the party obligated to pay them and taxable to the other party, and to what extent?
2) Whether certain other payments made for the other party's benefit (e.g., insurance premiums) are deductible as alimony?
3) Whether and to what extent there should be a differentiation between alimony to a spouse and child support?
4) Which party is eligible to claim a child dependency exemption?
5) Whether a transfer of property between the parties is a taxable transaction? And,
6) Under what conditions the parties are eligible to file a joint tax return.

* Never mind the occasional television and motion picture dramatization of couples locked in dramatic "property fights." The fact is this: studies on the matter show that it is the rare exception, not the rule, to find the divorcing couple with that much income or property to fight over. Usually, by the time of separation, or divorce especially, couples are already financially drained from such expenditures like legal costs and the costs of maintaining two household budgets in rents, food, housekeeping services, children's toys and clothing, medical coverage, utilities, transportation, magazines or newspapers, etc. As one New York Times investigator reported, "even for a moderate income divorced family... such a split can virtually overnight transform the family into two low-income households." (N.Y. Times, July 5, 1973 p. 43).

C. Tax Consequences In Matrimonial Decrees And Settlements Made Before January 1, 1985

1. Under the old previous law, marital support payments (alimony and maintenance) to be acceptable, had to be "periodic" payments — that is, they had to be paid in fixed amounts per week or month. And lump-sum payments were generally not acceptable. Furthermore, under the old law it was required that the payment made must be on account of a marital obligation imposed under local law. And only if these requirements were met, did the Internal Revenue Code (the tax law) allow such payments made in settlement of marital and support obligations to be a deductible expenditure in the payer's (mostly the husband's then as now) income tax returns, and similarly considered taxable income to the receiving spouse (generally the wife).

Under the old law, if a spouse (say the husband) makes ***support payments to the other spouse*** (say the wife), the payments will be generally deductible to him in his separate tax return and included within the gross income of the recipient spouse under these three conditions:

(a) That the payments he made are specifically required by a court decree of divorce, separation or separate maintenance, or by a written separation or settlement agreement.
(b) That the payments are made in relation to a legal marital relationship; and
(c) That the payments are "periodic" (or "semi-periodic"), as defined by the Internal Revenue Code.*

In brief, generally speaking alimony payments made either terminable or subject to change in the case of death, remarriage, or change in the economic structure of either party, were deemed "periodic". The contingent event may be provided either by the court decree or agreement or by state law. It is not essential that the "periodic" alimony be paid in equal amounts or at regular intervals.

There is one exception where, by a special provision of the Internal Revenue Code, even if the amount paid is not an "indefinite amount" (i.e., even if it is a lump sum payment), the payment may still be allowed as a deductible item by the payer: where the amount, though not an indefinite sum, is to be paid in "installments" over a period of **more than** 10 years from the date of the agreement or court decree. Such payments are said to be "quasi periodic" payments which would therefore qualify as a deductible expenditure by the paying spouse.

Thus, an agreement between a husband and wife whereby the husband is to pay the wife a fixed sum, say $100,000, in monthly equal installments but through a period of just 9 years and 11 months from the date of the agreement, will not qualify as a **"periodic" or "quasi-periodic" payment** — it will not be tax deductible by the husband (which also means that it would not be a taxable income to the wife who receives the payment). However, if the $100,000 were to have been similarly paid to the wife in fixed installments *but* OVER a period of 10 years and 1 month (more than 10 years), the payments would have fully qualified for tax deduction by the husband (and will also be taxable as income to the wife).

In this case, though, there is one qualification: the alimony payments will be deemed "periodic" alright, but deductions are limited in this case to a maximum of 10 percent of the principal sum each year, and applies only to advance alimony payment but does not include arrearages.

2. Payments made (whether over a 10 year period or otherwise) which are not in satisfaction of the *obligated party's* marital obligations, but rather are in settlement of the *recipient* party's marital obligations, are not considered "alimony" and are not deductible. Also, advance payments of periodic alimony made voluntarily by a party — that is, payments made which are informally arranged between the wife and the husband, but had not been specifically ordered by a court or required by a separation or settlement agreement — may be considered as not in discharge of a legal obligation and, therefore, as not being a deductible expense for tax purposes under Section 71 and 215 of the Internal Revenue Code.

---

* Periodic payments are of two basic types: 1) payments of specific amounts from time to time over an "indefinite period of time" with payments stopping only when a specified contingency, such as a spousal death or remarriage, occurs (i.e., fixed amounts for indefinite period based on the happening or non-happening of an indefinite future event); or 2) payments of indefinite amounts, such as a specific percentage of the husband's salary, from time to time over a specific period, say 5, 10, or 15 years (an indefinite or changeable amount for a fixed period of time). For a payment to qualify as "periodic," it must be payable: (1) for an indefinite period of time; or (2) in an indefinite amount; or (3) over a period of more than 10 years.

Likewise, such "voluntary" alimony payments made by the obligated party after the recipient party has remarried, are not deductible by the payer, nor are they considered as income to the recipient party, since under the laws of most states the spouse's legal obligation to pay alimony automatically terminates upon the remarriage of the spouse unless otherwise provided in the divorce decree. However, if the obligated party continues to make payments by reason of the ignorance of the recipient party's remarriage, the payments may be taxable to the recipient party.

Payments to recipient party in satisfaction of marital obligation.
In addition to qualifying as "periodic," all deductible alimony payments must be paid as a result of the marital relationship according to one of the following forms:

(1) A decree of divorce, regardless of the date entered, which may include a written agreement incidental to such decree; or
(2) A written separation agreement executed after August 16, 1954 (no date on the agreement is required, and an oral agreement stipulated to in open court proceedings will satisfy a "written requirement"); or
(3) A decree for separate maintenance (including temporary orders) entered after March 1, 1954.

In each of the above instances, the couple must be living in a state of separation (where the husband and wife are residing in the same household, they are not considered to be living in a state of separation) and filing separate returns for the year in which the deduction is claimed. If a joint return is filed, the alimony is not deductible by the obligated party, and the payments will not be income to the recipient party. The written agreement, however, is not required to be legally enforceable.

Temporary alimony payments required by court order are deductible under the same rules as permanent alimony. However, payments made pursuant to an oral agreement before the divorce, not required by order of the court, are not deductible.

Effective for taxable years beginning after December 31, 1976, alimony payments will be treated as a deduction from gross income rather than as an itemized deduction.

D. Tax Consequences In Matrimonial Decrees & Agreements Made After December 31, 1984

Under the new law (Tax Reform Act of 1984), the requirement that the alimony and separate maintenance payments must be made on account of a marital obligation imposed under local law has been repealed, and the requirement that the payment be "periodic" has been eliminated. The parties may designate in the instrument that otherwise qualifying alimony payments are to be nondeductible by the payor and excludable by the payee. The alimony and separate maintenance rules apply to divorce or separation instruments executed after December 31, 1984. The law also applies to any divorce or separation instrument executed before January 1, 1985, but modified on or after that date if the modification expressly provides that the provisions of the Act are to apply. The Tax Reform Act of 1986 amendments apply generally to instruments executed after December 31, 1986. It also applies to any divorce or separation instrument executed before January 1, 1987, but modified on or after that date, if the modification expressly provides that the provisions of the law are to apply.

Alimony and separate maintenance payments are deductible by the payor and are included within the gross income of the payee under the following conditions:

a) The payments must be made in cash;[1]

---

[1] I.R.C.ξ 71 (b) (1). Only cash payments, including checks and money orders payable on demand, qualify as alimony payments. Transfers of property, services, a debt instrument of a third party, an annuity contract, or use of property of the payor, etc., do not qualify. Thus, a party who transfers property, such as a vehicle, in satisfaction of alimony, would receive no deduction. Payments of rent, mortgage, liabilities, taxes, medical expenses, school tuition, or other expenses, qualify as alimony, provided payment is made pursuant to a divorce or separation instrument. See ξ 16-3, infra.

b) the payments must be made to the payee (or a third party for the payee's benefit) under a divorce or separation instrument;
c) Liability for payments must terminate at the death of the payee spouse;[2]
d) The divorce or separation instrument must state that there is no liability to make payments for any period after the death of the payee spouse;[3]
e) the parties, where separated under a decree of divorce or of separate maintenance (as distinguished from a separation agreement or decree for support), must not be members of the same household at the time of payment; the parties must not designate the payment as not being alimony, such as designating it as support for the children; and if any amount specified in the instrument will be reduced on the happening of a contingency relating to a child (e.g., reaching a specified age, marrying, dying, leaving school, or a similar contingency), then an equal amount will be treated as child support rather than alimony. (Example: if the divorce decree provides that payments will be reduced by $100 per month when a child reached age 18, then $100 of each monthly payment will be treated as fixed for child support).

In addition to the foregoing requirements, under the Tax Reform Act of 1986, any payments in excess of $15,000 during any calendar year will be deductible only if the divorce or separation instrument provides that the payor is required to make alimony payments for at least three consecutive calendar years beginning with the year a payment is first made (assuming neither spouse dies during that period and that the payee does not remarry); and the payments may not vary by more than $15,000 a year, or the excess payments (i.e., those earlier year payments in excess of the sum of the later year payments plus $15,000) will be includeable in the income of the payor and deductible by the payee in the subsequent year.[4]

There is no alimony income or deduction if the parties choose to file a joint return. The payee must furnish the payor with his or her social security number and the payer must furnish the name and social security number of the payee to the Internal Revenue Service.

E. Alimony: Indirect Payments

One area where the Tax Reform Act of 1984 (TRA '84) completely rewrote the tax laws relating to alimony and separate maintenance payments, is with respect to *indirect* alimony payments.
benefit and it will qualify as deductible so long as the other conditions[5] for the payments to qualify as deductible are met. Thus, assuming all other conditions are met, payments of the following to third persons for the benefit of the

---

2 There must be no liability to make any payment in cash or property as a substitute for such payments. I.R.C.ξ 71 (b) (1) (D); Treas. Reg ξ 1.71-1T (b)(A-10)

Under the Tax Reform Act of 1986, ξ 1981, payments must still be terminable upon the death of the dependent spouse. However, it is no longer necessary to make an explicit statement that the payments are terminable on death. If the payments are terminable by reason of state law (as they are, for example, in a state like North Carolina), they are deductible to the payor and taxable to the payee even though no explicit statement is made. This change is retroactive to the date of enactment of the Tax Reform Act of 1984. It is now appropriate for taxpayers to file amended returns claiming the deductions for 1985 or 1986 if the deductions were disallowed for failure to make an explicit statement. It is also necessary for the dependent spouse to file an amended return including the payments in income.

3 I.R.C.ξ 71 (b) (1) (D). The 1986 Tax Reform Act has modified this requirement so that although it is still necessary that the payments actually terminate at the payee's death, it is not necessary for the document to state such. But a good prudent practice is still to state in the document the intention of the parties as to taxability and deductibility.

4 The recapture provisions of the 1984 Act were altered by the Tax Reform Act of 1986, ξ1843. The new law (the 1986 law) applies to instruments executed on or after January 1, 1987, and reduces recapture only to three years instead of six under the previous Tax Reform Act of 1984; recapture occurs only in the three post-separation years; and there is a $15,000 cushion instead of a $10,000 cushion. The recapture rules under the 1986 Act are illustrated as follows:

(1) If payments for the second year exceed payments for the third year by more than $15,000, the excess is recaptured in the third year. For example, under a 1987 agreement, husband made payments to the wife in 1987 and 1988 of $30,000, and payments in 1989 are $10,000. Since the 1988 payments exceeded 1989 payments by $ 20,000 , the excess over $15,000 (or $5,000) is ordinary income to the husband in 1989 and not income to wife in 1989.
(2) If payments for the first year exceed the average of payments for the second and third year by more than $15,000, the excess over $15,000 is recaptured in the third year. For example, under a 1987 agreement, husband makes payments to wife in 1987 of $50,000, payments of $22,000 in 1988 and of $14,000 in 1989. The average payments for the second and third years is $18,000. Since 1989 payments exceed the average of 1988 and 1989 payments by $32,000, the excess over $15,000 ($17,000) is ordinary income to husband in 1989 and not income to the wife in 1989.
(3) If both of the rules above apply, the amount recaptured under the first rule is subtracted from second year payments for purposes of applying the second rule. For example, under a 1989 instrument, husband makes payments to wife in 1987 of $50,000 in 1988 of $40,000, and 1989 of $20,000. Under the first rule, second-year payments exceed third-year payments by $20,000, thus the excess over $15,000 ($5,000) is recaptured. To apply the second rule, the $5,000 recaptured under the first rule is subtracted from 1988 payments. Therefore, the average of 1988 and 1989 payments is $27,500. Payments in 1987 exceed the average of 1988 and 1989 payments by $22,500; thus the excess over $15,000 (7,500) is recaptured under the second rule. Therefore the total recapture is $12,500 — $5,000 under the first rule and $7,500 under the second rule.
The tax reform Act of 1986 allows parties to modify instruments executed in 1985 and 1986 that the recapture provisions of the new law, rather than that of the 1984 law, will be applicable.

5 See Sections C&D above.

payee spouse (or ex-spouse) would be deductible: medical expenses, house or rental payments, real estate taxes, insurance and home improvements, utilities, life insurance premiums, school tuition, the recipient spouse's income tax on alimony payments, and under certain limited conditions, attorney's fee.[6]

Apparently, life insurance proceeds, payments of trust corpus (but not the trust income), annuity payments, and payments made to maintain property owned by the payor spouse and used by the payee spouse, will not be subject to alimony treatment.[7]

F. Tax Treatment of Child Support

As explained in the preceding sections of this chapter, the tax Reform Act of 1984 (TRA '84) completely rewrote the tax laws relating to *alimony and separate maintenance payments*. The story, however, is totally different with respect to the tax treatment of *child support* payments: here, there's no change in the law, with the exception of the overruling of the decision in Commissioner v. Lester [366 U.S. 299, 81 S. Ct. 1343, 6L. Ed.2d 306 (1961)], as discussed below.

With respect to **child support,** payments made for child support which are the terms of a divorce decree or separation agreement, are treated exactly in the opposite way from payments made for the support of a spouse. Child support expenditures by the spouse or parent are *not* a tax deductible expense by the payor, and are *not* taxable income to the payee spouse — that is, the spouse or party (or even the child himself) who collects such payments does not pay tax on such receipts; they are not deductible by the payer, nor are they includable in the gross income of the payee (the party collecting it on behalf of the child). In such cases, if and when a payment is less than the amount specified in the divorce or separation instrument, it will be applied first to the required child support, and then any remainder to alimony; i.e., there is no pro rata division between child support and alimony.

On the other hand, suppose the payor makes a lump-sum payment for alimony and child support and does not specify what portion of the support payment is "child support"? In that event, the entire amount will be treated as alimony, assuming it otherwise qualifies, unless the parties have designated otherwise by written agreement. For example, the parties to an agreement may designate in the instrument that the alimony payments are to be non-deductible by the payor and excludable by the payee. However, if any amount specified in the instrument will be reduced on the happening of a contingency event relating to a child (e.g., the attainment of a specified age, marrying, dying, leaving school, etc.), then an equal amount will be treated as child support rather than alimony.[8] For example, if the divorce instrument provides that payments will be reduced by $100 per month when a child reaches age 18, then $100 of each monthly payment will be treated as fixed for child support and thus not deductible by the payer nor treated as income to the payee.

> **NOTE:** To be absolutely on the safe side, it is advised that the provisions of a settlement or separation agreement, or of a court decree, always clearly identify and ***differentiate*** any payments which are meant for child support, from those that are for the wife's support (alimony), if any. Support provisions should *not* be lumped together in a clause like: "The husband shall pay the sum of $200 per month for alimony and child support." Rather, a specific breakdown of how much is meant for the children's support and what part is meant for alimony, if applicable, should be exactly given. Lumping the payments together has had a long history of causing a lot of complications for both spouses with the Internal Revenue Service. [In one case, for example, the tax court

---

[6] The general rule is that attorney's fees are not deductible by either party, since they are considered to be personal expense. I.R.C. ξ 262. However, there are few well-defined exceptions. A recipient party may deduct expenses for attorney's fees incurred for the "production or collection of alimony." I.R.C. 212 (1). However, the recipient party must be prepared to show what proportion of the attorney's fees is attributable to the collection of alimony. In Re: Mirsky, 56T.C. 664. Both parties may deduct any portion of their attorney's fees attributable to tax advise. I.R.C. 212 (3). Adequate records must be kept showing what part of attorney's fees are attributable to tax advice. Hall v. U.S., 78-1 U.S.T.C. para. 9126 (Ct. Cl. 1977). However, except as provided above, the legal costs of prosecution or defending a divorce action are not deductible by either party, since it is presumed that the litigation arose from a personal as opposed to a business relationship. U.S. v. Gilmore, 372 U.S. 39. 83 S. Ct. 623, 9 L. Ed. 2d 577) (1963); U.S. v. Patrick, 372 U.S. 53, 83 S. Ct. 618, 9 L. Ed. 2nd 580 (1963). The obligated party's payment of the recipient party's attorney's fees is not deductible, unless it can otherwise qualify.

[7] See TRA '84 ξ421 (B) (2), repealed I.R.C. ξ101 (e), which made life insurance proceeds taxable to the payee spouse (or ex-spouse) as alimony. I.R.C. ξ682 and H.Rpt. 98-432 (Part 3) at p. 1492; TRA '84, ξ421 (b) (1), repealed I.R.C. ξ72 (k), which made annuity payments subject to alimony treatment; and Treas. Reg. ξ1.71 (b) (A-6).

[8] This derives from Tax Reform Act of 1984 422 (a) [I.R.C. S. 71 (c)(2)], overruling Commissioner v. Lester, 366 U.S. 299, 81 S. Ct.1343, 6L. Ed.306 (1961).

ruled that a wife who used payments designated as "alimony" to support the children in their custody, was entitled to claim them as her dependents for tax purposes.]

Historically, tax laws have made it advantageous for the parties to allow all or a major part of support payment to be treated as alimony, since the recipient party was typically in a lower income tax bracket than the obligated party. Due to the tax savings, the obligated party could afford to pay a larger sum as alimony, and the recipient party's higher income tax would normally be more than offset by the increase in alimony payments. Generally, careful planning can obtain these same advantages under the new laws. However, any such planning must take into consideration the strict requirements of the new tax laws (see Sections D & E above). Any such planning should also take into consideration which party will claim the child dependency exemption for each of the minor children.

Apparently there is nothing in the new tax law which would prevent the parties from modifying the divorce or separation instrument in order to effect a more advantageous tax treatment, but based on past rulings, the change will apply only to prospective (future) payments.

G. Treatment With Respect To Dependency Exemptions For Children

Tax Laws relating to dependency for children is another aspect that was completely rewritten by the Tax Reform Act of 1984 (TRA of 1984). Under the prior Law, while payments specifically designated as ***"Child Support"*** were, then as now, neither a taxable income to the payee-spouse nor a deductible expenditure to the paying spouse, the paying spouse may, however, be entitled to claim the children as his ***"dependents"***, which would then entitle him to take the $1,000 per dependent child "exemption" credit in his income tax return. A paying spouse did not, however, automatically qualify to take this dependency exemption; rather, the qualifying spouse entitled to claim a child as a dependent was the one who met the following requirements:

(a) If the child received the greater part of his support (over 50%) from his divorced or separated parents, then the child will be considered the dependent of that particular parent who has custody of him for *more than* 6 months of the calendar year.

(b) If the parties had a court order or a separation agreement which expressly provides, however, that the non-custodial parent (the one who does not have custody) would be entitled to the dependency exemption if he should contribute at least $600 towards the support of the child per year, then the provision or the court ,order or agreement would prevail. A spouse (say the father) would, in such a case be entitled to the exemption *providing* he paid $600 (or more) per child in child support for the year.

(c) If there was no court order or a valid agreement, or if the court order or agreement said nothing about the $600 provision mentioned above, then the non-custodial parent was nevertheless entitled to the exemption if he provided at least $1,200 in child support per child in a given year. The only way the custodial mother, rather than the non-custodial father, would be entitled to the exemption under such a circumstance, would be by showing a "clear evidence" that she contributed more than the husband did in support of the child for that year.

In short, under the prior law, to qualify for the $1,000-per-dependent child-exemption, the parent had to provide over one-half of the dependent's support, and there were special rules where the parents were divorced or separated.

Under the new law, however, beginning January 1, 1985, the new law provides that the "custodial parent"(defined as that parent who has custody for the greater portion of the calendar year), will be entitled to the exemption in all cases unless he or she waives the exemption by written declaration and the non-custodial parent attaches the declaration (I.R.S. Form 8332) to his or her tax return. In certain cases, pre-1985 decrees and agreements (unless amended) will continue under the same rules as prior law.

(1) Qualified pre-1985 decrees and agreements. Any "qualified" pre-1985 instrument (defined as any decree of divorce or separation maintenance or written agreement signed before 1/1/85, which provides that the non-custodial parent is entitled to claim the dependency exemption, and is not modified to provide that this exemption will not apply to it) will continue under the prior law whereby the non-custodial parent will be entitled to claim the $1,000 dependency exemption[9] (i) if he or she contributes at least $600.00 to the support of the child during the calendar year; (ii) if the "qualified" instrument proves that the non-custodial parent will be entitled to this exemption; (iii) if the child receives over half of his support during the calendar year from the parents; (iv) if the child is in the custody of one or both of his parents for more than one-half of the calendar year; and (v) if the parents are divorced or legally separated under a decree of divorce or separate maintenance, or are separated under a written separation agreement, or have lived apart at all times during the last six months of the calendar year.

(2) Taxable years beginning AFTER December 31, 1984. Except for "qualified" pre-1985 instruments (see definition above) for taxable years after December 31, 1984, in all cases the custodial parent (that parent who has custody for the greater part of the calendar year) will be entitled to the $1,000 dependency exemption[10] unless he or she signs a written declaration (IRS Form 8332) that such custodial parent will not claim the child as a dependent for any taxable year beginning in such calendar year and the non-custodial parent attaches the declaration to his or her tax return for the taxable year beginning during such calendar year. Furthermore, for the exemption to be available to either parent, the child must receive over half of his support during a calendar year from the parents; the child must be in the custody of one or both of his parents for more than one-half of the calendar year; and the parents must be either divorced or legally separated under a divorce decree or separate maintenance, or written agreement, or lived apart at all times during the last six months of the calendar year.

Since the Internal Revenue Code now requires an express waiver of the dependency exemption by the custodial parent, there is conflicting authority as to whether the court has the authority to allocate the dependency exemption to a parent. The court has three basic options: it may allocate the exemption, order the custodial spouse to execute a written declaration waiving the exemption, or refuse to do either. Public policy in creating more income to pay support would, however, support the court's allocation to the payor spouse. The exemption may also be a property right to be allocated by equitable distribution.

(3) Miscellaneous. As under present law, the foregoing rules will not apply in the case of multiple support agreements under the new tax law. For purposes of the medical expenses deduction, a child who is subject to the above rules will be treated as a dependent of both parents. By waiving the right to claim the dependent exemption, the custodial parent does not lose eligibility for head of household status, child care credit, nor earned income credit.

H. Transfers Of Property

The Tax Reform Act of 1984 [I.R.C. ξ1015; ξ104; ξ1239], completely rewrote the tax laws relating to transfers of property incident to a divorce. Generally, after July 18, 1984, property transfers between the parties because of a divorce will no longer be a taxable event (repealing U.S. v. Davis, 370 U.S. 65, 82 S. Ct. 1190, 8 L. Ed. 2d 335 [1962]). The transfer will be treated for income tax purposes in the same manner as a gift. The transferor will have no recognized gain or loss, and the transferee will receive the property at the transferor's basis. However, prior law will continue to apply to transfers pursuant to a divorce decree or separation agreement in effect on the date of enactment of the new law (July 18, 1984), unless both parties elect to have the rules apply to such transfers.

(1) Transfers of property pursuant to instruments in effect PRIOR TO July 18, 2984. Unless both parties elect to have the new rules apply, prior law will continue to apply to transfers made pursuant to divorce decree or separation agreement in effect prior to July 18, 1984. [Note that the Tax Reform Act of 1986 eliminated the capital gains rates]. Accordingly, if the transferor transfers appreciated property to the transferee as alimony, or otherwise transfers it in discharge of marital rights, the transferor will realize a gain subject to taxation under the usual rules. Whether the gain will be taxed as ordinary income or capital gain depends upon the character of the property

9 The $1,000 is subject to a cost-of-living adjustment. The Tax Reform Act of 1986 increased the dependency exemptions to $1,900 in 1987, $1,950 in 1988, and $2,000 in 1989 and subsequent years. If the spouse paying child support has taxable income which exceeds $149,250 on a joint return, $89,560 on a single return, and $123,790 on a head of household return, it may be advisable to allocate the dependency exemption to the recipient spouse, since the 1989 Tax Reform Act ξ1(g), recaptures the entire benefits of the exemptions at such income levels.

10 The dependent is the parent's "child" as defined in I.R.C. ξ151 (e) (3) (biological child, stepchild, legally adopted child) where the child has not reached age 19 before the close of the taxable year. Note that where there is no award of legal custody, physical custody is the determining factor. See Treas. Reg. ξ1-152-4(b)

transferred. The amount of the gain is the difference between the transferor's adjusted basis for the property and the fair market value at the time of the transfer.

A clear distinction should be drawn between a property settlement, whereby the parties simply divide their jointly owned property, and a transfer in satisfaction of the transferee's inchoate marital rights. In the case of a strict property division, there is no taxable event and no tax. On the other hand, where the transferor transfers property to the transferee in consideration of the latter's claim for alimony, any gain realized by the transferor is subject to taxation. In other words, in such a situation the controlling criterion is the intent of the parties rather than the designation placed on the transfer.

The transferee is not considered to have realized a gain in the release of his or her claim for alimony, and any assets which he or she receives in the transaction will have the current fair market value as a basis for future transfers.

(2) **Transfers of property subject to the law.** Under I.R.C ξ47 (e), there are three types of transfers between spouses or incident to a divorce subject to the 1984 law: (i) transfers made after the Law's date of enactment (July 18, 1984) (other than transfers pursuant to an instrument in effect prior thereto); (ii) transfers after the law's date of enactment (July 18, 1984) pursuant to an instrument then in effect, if both parties elect to have the new rules apply to the transfer; and (iii) transfers after December 31, 1983, if both parties elect to have the new rules apply to the transfer, per new IRS regulations.

The 1984 law overrules United States v. Davis, and provides that no gain or loss will be recognized on a transfer of property between spouses or between former spouses if the transfer is incident to a divorce. The property transferred will be treated as acquired by the transferee by gift, and the basis of the transferee in the property will be the adjusted basis of the transferor. A transfer of property is incident to a divorce if such transfer (1) occurs within one year after the date on which the marriage ceases or (2) is related to the cessation of the marriage.

The new rules also apply to transfer in trust, transfers of annuities, transfers of life insurance contracts, and transfers of installment obligations.

As a general rule, benefits under a tax deferred retirement plan cannot be assigned or alienated without the possible loss of deferred tax benefits. Because of the need to transfer retirement benefits incident to divorce, the Internal Revenue Service created an exception to the general rule. This rule continued until the passage of the Retirement Equity Act of 1984. The 1984 law allows the transfer of retirement benefits, provided the parties meet the requirements for a ***Qualified Domestic Relations Order (QDRO).*** When the requirements are met, the benefits are afforded favorable tax treatment, and the plan remains tax deferred.

I. Miscellaneous Provisions

The Tax Reform Act of 1984, made many miscellaneous changes to the tax laws relating to married persons and divorced persons. Generally, these rules were effective after December 31, 1984.

(1) Head of household status. A party may qualify for a lower income tax rate as a "head of household" if he is not married at the end of a taxable year and maintains a household within the meaning of I.R.C. ξ2 (b). For tax years prior to 1985, the taxpayer's household must be the residence of the child for the entire taxable year for the taxpayer to qualify as head of the household. Beginning with the taxable year 1985, the new law requires only that the household be the child's principal residence only for more than one-half of the taxable year.

(2) Joint return. A joint return may not be filed by parties who are divorced or separated under a decree of separate maintenance, since they would be considered for tax purposes as unmarried. Neither may a husband or wife file joint returns while one spouse claims alimony payments as deductions. Of course, the filing of a joint return renders both spouses jointly and severely liable for all due taxes, but the 1984 law liberalized the *"innocent spouse rule"* in that, under certain conditions, a spouse may be relieved of liability for a substantial understatement of tax on a joint return that is attributable to the grossly erroneously items of the other spouse.

(3) Individual retirement accounts. Under the 1984 tax law, alimony or separate maintenance payments qualify for purposes of computing contributions to an individual retirement account (IRA).

(4) Federal estate tax. For estates of persons dying after July 18, 1984, the obligation to transfer property to a former spouse of the deceased will be deductible as a claim against the estate if the transfer is pursuant to an agreement which satisfies certain conditions.

(5) Federal gift tax. For transfers of property to a former spouse in consideration of the release of that spouse's marital rights, prior law provided that if certain conditions were met, there would be no taxable gift. For gifts made after July 18, 1984, to a former spouse, the new law liberalizes the conditions under which a transfer would not be a taxable gift.

(6) Attorney's fees. Generally, legal services rendered in connection with divorce and other marital issues are deemed to be "personal" rather than business-related, and are therefore not deductible. However, an individual is allowed to deduct all the ordinary and necessary expenses paid or incurred:

(1) for the production or collection of income;

(2) for the management, conservation, or maintenance of property held for the production of income; or

(3) in connection with the determination, collection, or refund of any tax. Thus, legal expenses attributable to the production or collection of taxable alimony are deductible by the recipient of the alimony. (IRS ξ31.262-1). Legal fees for the conservation or maintenance of property held for the production of income in the divorce setting have generally failed.[11] Legal fees incurred for tax research and advice in connection with a divorce and property settlement are deductible.[12] Beginning in 1987, otherwise deductible legal fees will be deductible as "any other miscellaneous itemized deduction" only to the extent that they exceed two percent of the adjusted gross income of the taxpayer.

---

11 See U.S. v. Gilmore, 372 U.S. 39, 83 S. Ct. 623, 9L. Ed. 2d 570 (1963)

12 Carpenter v. U.S., 338 F. 2d 366 (Ct. Cl. 1964); Rev Rul. 72-545, 1972-2 C.B. 179; U.S. v. Davis, 370 U.S. 65, 82, S. Ct. 1190, 8 L. Ed. 2d 335, reh. den., 371 U.S. 854, 83 S. Ct. 14, 9 L. Ed. 2d 92 (1962).

APPENDIX A

FINANCIAL STATEMENT OF NET WORTH **Date Made:**________________

Made by Mr/Mrs ________________________________

A. *List Your Assets*

Real Estate (land, home, business property, condos, co-ops, etc.)

Description or address | Type of ownership (sole, joint, etc) | Market Value Equity

____

____

____

Cash or Equivalent Funds (checking accounts, savings accounts money market accounts, certificates of deposit, etc.)

Bank | Account Type & Number | Balance

____

____

____

Investments (stocks, bonds, mutual fund shares, CD's other securities, etc.)

Type | Company | Number of shares | Market Value

____

____

____

Personal Property

List major items of personal property owned (including furs, jewelry, art, cash on hand, all items of substantial value):

____

____

____

Other Personal Property—whatever you own (furniture's, clothes, etc.) that are not major. (You need not list individual items unless of significant value)

Description | Approx. Value

____

____

____

MARKED: EXHIBIT ___________

Automobiles — List all interests in automobiles

Type License Number Insurance Company

Retirement Plans (IRS's profit sharing, pension plans, Keoghs, etc.)

Type Name of Plan Beneficiary Current Value

Life Insurance (also note the policy number and type of insurance coverage, such as "whole" or "term")

Insured Person Company 1st Beneficiary 2nd Beneficiary Death Benefit

Accounts/Notes Receivable & Debts owed you (include name, address and phone number)

Who owes Amount owed you

Special items of value (items of substantial value, e.g., coin collections, antiques, jewelry, art, etc.)

Description Approx. value

B. *List Your Liabilities*

Type *Company/Persons owed* *Amount owed* *When due* *Secured by*

Mortgages

Installment Loans (credit cards, etc.)

Education Loans

Personal Loans

Taxes owed

Other debts

C. *Figuring Out Your Net Worth*

AMOUNTS

Yours Joint (if any)

ASSETS

Real Estate

Cash or Equivalent Funds

Investments ______________________________
Personal Property ______________________________
Other Personal Property ______________________________
Automobiles ______________________________
Retirement Plans ______________________________
Life Insurance ______________________________
Accounts Rec./Debts owed to you ______________________________
Special items of value ______________________________
Deferred compensation (income earned but not received) ______________________________
***Total Assets* ....(A)** ______________________________

LIABILITIES

Mortgages ______________________________
Installment Loans ______________________________
Education Loans ______________________________
Personal Loans ______________________________
Taxes owed ______________________________
Other debts ______________________________
____

***Total Liabilities* ....(B)** ______________________________

NET ESTATE .... ______________________________
(assets minus liabilities)
(A)— (B)

Submitted By: **X**______________________________
(signature of maker)

A Copy is Hereby Acknowledged Received By: **X**______________________________ on __________
(signature of partner) (date)

APPENDIX B

The Basic Procedure of Dividing Up Retirement Benefits Between Couples, And Meeting the QDRO Requirements

An employee pension could often be a couple's biggest asset, and in modern times retirement benefits are one special type of PERSONAL PROPERTY which divorcing or separating couples will have to agree upon. (See Chapter 3 at p. 15-17 for a detailed treatment of this.) The important question here is: assuming that, during your marriage, one or both spouses have accrued the right to some day receive a retirement benefit as a result of employment (or military service), how do you place a value on it and divide it up equitably in your settlement agreement or divorce?

Distribution Options

For simplicity and brevity, there are two basic ways you can divide pension benefits:

Option #1: You can elect to let the current owner of the pension benefit (the covered employee spouse) keep the full benefits and to give the other spouse cash or other assets worth half the <u>current</u> value of the part of the benefits accrued during the marriage, (The employee spouse could, for example, keep his full pension but waive his rights to a jointly-owned home, and in return, the other spouse would receive full title to the house but also waive all her rights to the pension).

This option, however, requires that you be able to figure out what the *current value* of the benefits is so as to be able to apportion the benefits. In practice, you'll have to hire an actuary (a pension or insurance evaluation specialist) who'll be better able to make the proper computations, and can, through swapping the present value of the unemployed spouse's share of the pension with other marital property, place a present value on the pension. And, with such a figure, the pension can then be divided fairly as agreed to between the spouses, in terms of whether the state is based on the maniple equitable distribution or on community property principle.

Option #2: Alternatively, you can give the non-employee spouse the right to receive part of the retirement benefits when those benefits are eventually paid out — i.e., upon the employee spouse's retirement.

Under this option, it is not necessary to figure out the <u>current</u> value of the benefits; both spouses will simply have to wait to receive any payments until the employee-spouse is eligible to receive the benefits. *However, here's an important point: if you choose this option, your settlement agreement with your spouse must generally contain appropriate provisions for what is known as a "Qualified Domestic Relations Order" (QDRO), and such an agreement must also be filed with, and be accepted by the official administrator of the subject retirement plan for it to be effective.*

Qualified Domestic Relations Order Or QDRO

What is a Domestic Relations Order (QDRO, for short)? A "domestic relations order" is a court order which creates or recognizes the existence of an alternate payee's (a former spouse's, child's or other dependent's) right to, or assigns to him or her the right to, receive the benefits payable to a participant in a retirement plan. And a domestic relations order is "qualified" if it clearly specifies certain requirements as set forth under Section 414 (p) of the Retirement Equity Act of 1984 (such as the name and particulars of the participant and each alternate payee covered by the order, the amount or percentage of benefits payable to each alternate payee, the number of payments affected or the period to which the order applies, and identification of each plan to which the order applies, etc.) But, more simply defined, a QDRO is a court-signed order which, upon it's being signed at the time of a divorce, and then being "qualified" by the administrator of the pension plan to make certain it meets the plan's requirements, then splits the pension according to the marital couple's property settlement agreement.

QDRO is necessary because, legally, a pension belongs only to the participant in the pension plan —that is, the covered employee—spouse. Therefore , to divide a pension, a court issues such an order —the QDRO, basically directed at the administrator of the pension plan to get him to treat the other spouse just as if he or she were equally a participant in the plan.

Q.D.R.O's were authorized by the Retirement Equity Act of 1984, which addressed the spousal rights of a pension. Prior to that time, it was possible to split pension benefits in divorce by a court order, but any such court order was directed at *the spouse with the pension,* rather than at the *pension plan itself.* For example, the husband might be directed by the court that once he began to receive a monthly pension, say some 10 to 15 years in the future, he should be sending one-half of that to his former wife. That old system, however, often left many spouses pensionless, in that under those conditions, if the former husband died before retirement, the ex-wife received nothing. Consequently, under the 1984 law (which became effective on January 1, 1985), it is *the pension Plan Administrator,* as opposed to the spouse with the pension, that is ordered to see to it that the other spouse gets the share of the pension plan that is due her; the plan administrator is ordered, basically, to treat the non-pensioned spouse just as if he or she were equally a participant in the pension plan.

Q.D.R.O.s Apply To Defined Benefit & Defined Contribution Plans, Only

First, you should note that the QDRO orders apply only to "defined benefit" and "defined contribution" plans like 401(k) and profit-sharing plans. They do not apply to Individual Retirement Accounts or special arrangements that companies set up for high-paid executives.

In an order involving, for example, a defined benefit plan, where the benefit amount is not determined until the participant's retirement, an actuarial formula might be used in the order to divide the pension. A clause such as this, for example, might be provided in the order: "Upon the retirement of my spouse, I will get one-half of his pension, which benefits will continue for my lifetime." On the other hand, if it were a defined contribution plan — like a 401(K), which has a specified dollar amount — the plan might be split in half as of the divorce date.

Procedure Relating To The Drafting Of the Order

FIRST: Because retirement plans vary, contact the administrator of the retirement plan in question. Ask for the following:

1. copies of any available written summary of the plan, copies of the retirement plan, preferably;
2. a statement of the value of the employee's expected benefits;
3. The requirements or items that should be covered by the settlement agreement and Order;
4. procedures for QDRO's;

5. any forms the administrator may have prepared. And in most instances, you would probably be able to get practical assistance and guideline from the plan administrator, as to what is acceptable, since it is with him that the agreement and order are to be filed, and he has to give his acceptance of the documents.

SECOND: In writing up your marital settlement agreement, you must be sure to enter therein the applicable agreements you shall have reached with your spouse on how the pension benefits are to be split — who is to be entitled to what benefits and when and how. [See Article 12, Part III, of the sample Marital Separation/Settlement Agreement on p. 53, for sample provisions].

THIRD: At the time of divorce, draw up the following papers, among others, and incorporate in such papers the terms of the agreements and understandings you have reached with your spouse regarding the pension benefits:

I. A Qualified Domestic Relations Order (see samples on p. 93&95); and
II. Determination of Qualification of Pension Plan by Plan Administrator (see sample on p. 94).

Basically, a QDRO should be tailored to comply with the parties' agreement and the retirement Plan's provisions. The simple approach is this: simply follow, for your general guidance, the QDRO forms and format provided you by the administrator of the retirement plan involved.

FOURTH: A copy of QDRO order, upon being "issued" (signed) by the divorce court, will be served by the court upon the designated retirement plan administrator, who in turn is to notify both spouses of his receipt of the order.

The plan administrator then has 18 months, from the time the court issues the order, to examine the order and to determine if it meets the requirements of the law as being "qualified." Furthermore, the administrator is to notify the spouses of the procedure the plan will use in determining if the Order is "qualified." And, finally, the administrator formally serves notice on the spouse as to whether the Order is actually "qualified," and if not then the reasons for which it is not. (If an Order is not acceptable to the administrator, you will simply have to go back to court to get an order correcting the designated defects.)

In/For The ____________________ Court of the State of _________
County of _______________

Petitioner: ______________________________
Action/Index No. _________________________

VS.

Co-Petitioner/ _____________________________
Respondent _____________________________

Action/Index No. ______________

QUALIFIED DOMESTIC RELATIONS ORDER *(a sample)*

A Property Settlement Agreement providing for maintenance, child support and property division, having been executed by the parties on _______________ and filed herein on __________, which Agreement has been examined by this Court and found to be conscionable and in compliance with the laws of the State of __________, and the said Agreement having been incorporated into a Decree of Dissolution (Divorce) entered herein on ________,

And Motion having been made for a Qualified Domestic Relations Order to entitle the Alternate Payee, namely _______________, to receive benefits from the Participant's retirement plan as agreed upon by the parties

NOW, THEREFORE, IT IS ORDERED AS FOLLOWS;

The name of the plan hereby affected is ____
The name and address of the Participant in said plan is:

____
____
____
____

The Alternate Payee shall receive from said plan the sum of $________ (or percent of the amount payable to the participant) each month from the time the participant begins drawing periodic benefits, whether by disability or retirement, until the benefits payable under the said plan terminate. In the event of the participant's death prior to retirement, the alternative payee shall receive *(sum or percentage)* of the death benefits payable under the said plan. In the event the participant withdraws from the plan prior to retirement or death, for whatever reason, and receives proceeds from the plan by lump sum or otherwise, the alternate payee shall receive *(sum or percentage)* of the amount payable to the participant.

Upon receipt of a copy of the Order, the Plan administrator shall:

(a) notify the participant and the alternate payee of receipt of the copy;
(b) segregate the funds to which the participant would otherwise be entitled while it is being determined if this Order meets the requirements of the Retirement Equity Act of 1984 and is "qualified;"

(c) ensure that the participant may not borrow against the non-participant's share;
(d) notify the participant and the alternate payee of the procedure the plan will use to determine if this Order is "qualified;" and
(e) notify the participant and the alternate payee whether this Order is "qualified," and if not the reasons therefore.

IT IS FURTHER ORDERED that this Order may be amended or modified, if necessary, to permit it to become a "Qualified Domestic Relations Order" if it is determined that it does not initially comply with the requirements of the Equity Retirement Act of 1984 or any other law or laws dealing with this subject, so that the parties' intention of permitting the alternate payee to share in the plan can be accomplished.

ENTER: ______________________________
(Judge)

(Determination of Qualification by Plan Administrator.) (New)

*(Name of the Plan)*________________ **PENSION PLAN**
DETERMINATION OF QUALIFICATION

In compliance with Sections 104(a) and 204(a) of the Retirement Equity Act of 1984 (REA), which created Section 206(d)(3)(G)(i)(II) of the Employee Retirement Income Security Act of 1974 (ERISA), and Section 414(p)(6)(a)(ii) of the Internal Revenue Code of 1986, as amended, respectively, the undersigned Plan Administrator, on its own behalf and on behalf of its successors, does hereby determine that:

1. The attached Order is a Qualified Domestic Relations Order under ERISA and the Internal Revenue Code;
2. The Alternate Payee and Participant are to be notified of such qualification of the attached Order by receiving a copy of this determination; and
3. The undersigned Plan Administrator and its successors will comply with this Order.

Dated this _______ day of ________, 19__

____
(Name & Signature)

PLAN ADMINISTRATOR ______________________________

(full name of Plan Administrator) ______________________________

(full name of Plan) ______________________________

(address of Plan Administrator) ______________________________

Sample *Qualified Domestic Relations Order (QDRO)*
(Louisiana Version)

In The ____________ Court
For the Parish/County of ____________
State of ____________
Division ____________

Petitioner: ____________	**Case/Docket No.** ____________
VS.	
Co-Petitioner/ Respondent ____________ ____________	

Filed: ____________

____
Deputy Clerk

APPENDIX TO JUDGMENT:
DOMESTIC RELATIONS ORDER

IT IS ORDERED, ADJUDGED AND DECREED that ____________ shall receive payments from, and be designated as, and Alternate Payee of the ____________ *(Name of Plan)* ____________ Pension Plan and Trust Pursuant to the assignments of the benefits by ____________ to ________, pursuant to that certain Settlement of Community Property Agreement by and between ____________ and ____________, dated ________, 19__, in compliance with Sections 401 (a)(13) and 414 (p) of the Internal Revenue Code of 1986, as amended, as follows:

1. The Participant is ________ (hereinafter sometimes referred to as the "Participant"), whose Social Security Number is ________, and whose last known mailing address is ____________.

2. The Alternate Payee is __________ (hereinafter sometimes referred to as the "Alternate Payee"), whose Social Security Number is __________, and whose last known mailing address is ____________.

3. The Participant assigns to the Alternate Payee a portion of the benefits from the Participant's benefits from the following employee retirement benefit plan in which (*name of the participant-spouse*) is a participant, and the following employee retirement benefit plan shall pay benefits to the Alternate Payee as provided in this Order:

(Name of) Pension Plan and Trust

4. ___ # ______ years is the number of years during which the Participant was a participant of the *(Name of)* Pension Plan (the "Plan") during the existence of the community of acquets and gains between the Participant and the Alternate Payee.

5. The Plan from which benefits are assigned under Paragraph 3 above will pay benefits to the alternate Payee under the following formula:

$$\text{Benefit} = \frac{\#}{X} \times 1/2 \times \text{Accrued Benefit}^{**}$$

Accrued Benefit = The benefit that would be payable to the Participant at the earlier of (i) the Plan's normal retirement date, assuming the Participant terminated employment with the sponsor of the Plan at the normal retirement date or (ii) the date the Alternate Payee first begins receiving benefits under the Plan.

X The Participant's total number of years of plan participation, as determined in accordance with the provisions of the Plan as of the earlier of (i) actual termination of employment by the Participant or (ii) the date the Alternate Payee first begins receiving benefits under the Plan.

6. If benefits to the Participant commence at a pre-or-post normal retirement date, the Accrued Benefit shall be adjusted in light of the Plan actuarial factors relating to the early or deferred retirement date in effect at the time of benefit commencement.

7. If the Alternate Payee begins to receive benefits pursuant to this Order and the Participant subsequently retires with subsidized early retirement benefits, the amount payable to the Alternate Payee shall be recalculated as necessary, if necessary, so that the Alternate Payee shall receive a percentage of the subsidized benefits that the Participant is entitled to receive, based on the formula provided in Paragraph 5 above.

8. Under the Plan, the Participant shall elect a benefit form that provides a survivor benefit. The survivor benefit shall be a percentage of the benefit provided to the Participant during the Participant's life at least equal to that percentage determined by using the formula provided in Paragraph 5 above. The Participant shall designate the Alternate Payee as the beneficiary of this survivor benefit. The Alternate Payee shall be treated as the Participant's spouse for all purposes under the plan. As the surviving spouse, the Alternate Payee shall be entitled to any pre-retirement survivor annuity. The Alternate Payee's consent shall be required for any election of any benefits by the Participant other than the qualified pre-retirement or retirement joint and survivor annuity as provided under Section 417 of the Internal Revenue Code of 1986, as amended.

9. This assignment of benefits does not require the Plan to provide any type or form of benefit, or any option, not otherwise provided under the Plan. This assignment does not require the Plan to provide increased benefits (determined on the basis of actuary value). This assignment does not require the Plan to provide benefits to the Alternate Payee which are required to be paid to another Alternate Payee under another order previously determined to be a Qualified Domestic Relations Order.

10. The Participant, the Alternate Payee, and the Court, intend this Order to be a Qualified Domestic Relations Order as defined in Section 414(p) of the Internal Revenue Code of 1986, as amended.

11. The parties agree that their mutual intent is to provide the Alternate Payee with a retirement payment that fairly represents her marital share of the retirement benefits defined in Paragraph 3. If any order submitted to the administrator of the Plan is not held to be a Qualified Domestic Relations Order ("QDRO") within the meaning of Section 414(p) of the Internal Revenue Code of 1986, as amended, the parties agree to request a Court of competent

---

** This formula is appropriate for a "defined benefit" plan not currently in pay status and is based on the formula in Sims v. Sims, 358 So. 2d 919 (1978, La). A QDRO should be tailored to comply with the parties' agreement and the Plan's provisions. There's a different formula for a "defined contribution" plan.

jurisdiction to modify the Order to make it a QDRO that reflects the parties' intent, which modification Order shall be entered *nunc pro tunc* if appropriate.

__________________, Lousiana, this _________ day of _________. 19__.

____

JUDGE

APPROVED AS TO FORMAT AND CONTENT, AS SUBMITTED:

Name: ____________________________ Signature: ______________________________
(As and For Co-Petitioner/Respondent)

Name: ____________________________ Signature: ______________________________
(As and For Co-Petitioner/Respondent)

APPENDIX C

GROUNDS AND OTHER RELEVANT INFORMATION FOR OBTAINING A DIVORCE IN ALL 50 STATES & D.C.

As of the time of this writing, all 50 states in the nation have now adopted some form of "no-fault" law or procedure for dissolving marital relationships. This relatively recent development in matrimonial law administration has, in turn, translated into a big practical difference for the average divorce seeker across the nation.

The big difference is this: for *the first time in the nation's history, the standards and requirements for getting a divorce (the so-called "grounds") are now more or less uniform and standardized across the country!* Now, for the most part at least, all you'll practically need in order to file or be granted a divorce in just about any state, is to submit some form of a written statement* to your state's court making the claim that both spouses are in agreement that your marital relationship has absolutely failed or broken down. And hardly any judge or court official necessarily needs concern himself any more with whose "fault" it is, before you could be granted a divorce under such circumstances!

In view of this new reality, most Separation or Settlement agreements nowadays are ultimately used as a basis for final settlement in a divorce action [see Chapters 2 and 4 for a fuller treatment of this] Hence, it is hoped that couples or persons in every state would find the contents of this Appendix both relevant and helpful in planning their separation or divorce matters.

Included in this chapter, are the following information: the statutory "grounds" (reasons) for which divorce is allowed in each state; the court which handles divorce matters in each state; the title by which the state statutes (or laws) governing divorce is cited in each state; some clarifications or court interpretations of the laws in certain states; the principles by which marital property is allocated upon divorce** ; the state residency requirement for filing in each state, and identification of the 'no-fault' grounds for each state.

The actual procedures for filing for divorce are, of course, beyond the scope of this manual, and those interested in this may consult the volumes by the publisher, *How To Do Your Own Divorce Without A Lawyer*, authored by Benji O. Anosike. But, in general the procedures, especially for an "uncontested" divorce, are basically identical from state to state. It often boils down to one rather simple routine: securing a set of simple forms prescribed by the local court, filling them out, and submitting them to the appropriate state court for approval and the judge's signature.

NOTE: The companion manual, the 10-Volume *"How To Do Your Own Divorce Without A Lawyer"* series, published by The Selfhelper Law Press of America, a subsidiary of this publisher, provides the interested reader with the same facility to enable you undertake the procedures for actually filing for a divorce yourself. Included in each regional edition, which covers all the 50 states, are details of the actual procedures and sample forms for filing for divorce in each state, information on how to obtain the necessary filing forms, and other relevant details. Readers may write to the present Publisher for availability and price information.

---

* It doesn't matter whether your local court calls it a "petition," a "stipulation," a "verified complaint," or whatever. They're all generally one and the same thing.

** The rules by which marital property is divided up on divorce, fall into three different basic categories: 1) The "community property" states, in which spouses split *equally* all assets acquired by either or both parties (usually excluding those acquired before marriage, or by gift or inheritance); 2) the "equitable property" states, which make marital assets distributable to the spouses on the basis of justice and fair play determined on a case-by-case manner; and 3) the "common law" states, where ownership of property goes to the spouse who has legal title or his/her name to it at the time of divorce. Most states (as of this writing 48 of the 50 states) are now either community property or equitable property-based. [See Chapter 3 of the guidebook for more on this]

THE GROUNDS FOR A DIVORCE IN EACH STATE NOW FOLLOW.

ALABAMA

Grounds:

*1.) Voluntary separation for over 1 year; *2) Incompatibility of temperament so that parties can no longer live together; *3. Irretrievable breakdown of the marriage so that further attempts at reconciliation are impractical or unproductive; 4) Incurable physical incapacity to enter into the marital state at the time of the marriage; 5) Adultery; 6) Imprisonment (actual confinement) in a penitentiary for two years, under sentence for seven years or more; 7) Commission of a crime against nature before or after marriage; 8) Drug addiction or habitual drunkenness; 9) Confinement in an insane asylum for five successive years after marriage; 10) Pregnancy (by wife) caused by another man at the time of marriage; 11) living apart and non-support of wife by husband for two years (wife has to file).

Incompatibility is defined by court decisions as conflicts in personality and disposition that render it impossible for the parties to continue a normal marital relationship with each other. Lipham v. Lipham, 281 So. 2d 437.

Court: Circuit Court
Statute: Code of Alabama, Title 30
Residence: 1 year

ALASKA

Grounds:

*1. Incompatibility of temperament; *2. Failure to consummate the marriage at the time of marriage, and up to the time of the commencement of the divorce action; 3) Adultery; 4) Conviction of a felony; 5) Desertion for one year; 6) cruel and inhuman treatment; indignities against the other spouse; 7) Habitual drunkenness for one year prior to commencement of divorce action; 8) insanity or mental illness for which the spouse is confined to an institution for a period of at least eighteen months prior to commencement of the action; 9) Narcotic addiction.

Court: Superior Court
Statute: Alaska Statutes Annotated 09.55.110.
Residence: 1 year

ARIZONA

Grounds:

*1. A finding that the marriage is irretrievably broken (Defined as where there is no reasonable prospect of reconciliation).

Arizona Revised Statutes 25-314, states as follows, in part:

"The verified petition in a proceeding for dissolution of marriage or legal separation shall allege that the marriage is irretrievably broken or [that] one or both of the parties desire to live separate and apart, whichever is appropriate, and shall set forth:

"The verified petition in a proceeding for dissolution of marriage or legal separation shall allege that the marriage is irretrievably broken or one or both of the parties desire to live separate and apart, whichever is appropriate, an shall set forth:

1. The age, occupation and address of each party and the length of domicile in this state;
2. The date of the marriage and the place at which it was performed;
3. The names, ages and addresses of all living children, natural or adopted, common to the parties and whether the wife is pregnant;

---

* Indicates this is a "no-fault" ground.

4. The details of any agreements between the parties as to support, custody and visitation of the children and maintenance of spouse;
5. The relief sought."

Court: Superior Court
Property distribution rule upon divorce: By community property rule
Statute: Arizona Revised Statutes 25-312.
Residence: 1 year

ARKANSAS

Grounds:

*1) Living separate and apart for 18 consecutive months regardless of fault; marital misconduct relevant only when the wife seeks alimony or property division; 2) Impotence at the time of the marriage and up until commencement of the action; 3) Desertion for one year; 4) Prior existing marriage; 5) Conviction of a felony or other infamous crime; 6) Habitual drunkenness for one year prior to commencement of action; indignities to or cruel and inhuman treatment of the other spouse; 7) Adultery; 8) Living separate for three years because of the adjudicated insanity of the spouse, or because of his (her) confinement to an institution for 3 years prior to the action; 9) Willful non-support by spouse.

Court: Chancery Courts
Statute: Arkansas Statutes Annotated 34-1202.
Residence: 3 months

CALIFORNIA

Grounds:

*1) Irreconcilable differences, which have caused the irremediable breakdown of the marriage; 2) Incurable insanity.

The term "irreconcilable differences," has been interpreted as the existence of a level of marital problems which have impaired the marriage relationship to the point where the legitimate objects of matrimony have been destroyed and for which there is no reasonable possibility of elimination, correction or resolution. In re: Walton's Marriage, 104 Cal. Rptr. 472, 28 C.A. 3d 108.

Court: Superior Court
Property distribution rule upon divorce: By community property rule
Statute: California Civil Code 4506.
Residence: 6 months

COLORADO

Grounds:

*1) Irretrievable breakdown of the marriage.

According to the relevant section of the statute, this is how the term 'irretrievable breakdown', should be applied by the state courts: "If both of the parties by petition or otherwise have stated under oath or affirmation that the marriage is irretrievable broken, or one of the parties has so stated and the other has not denied it, there is a presumption of such fact, and, unless controverted by evidence, the court shall, after hearing, make a finding that the marriage is irretrievably broken."

Court: District Court
Statute: Colorado Revised Statutes 14-10-101.
Residence: 1 year

---

* Indicates this is a "no-fault" ground.

CONNECTICUT

Grounds:

*1) The marriage has broken down irretrievably and there is no reasonable prospect of reconciliation; *2) The parties have lived apart for a continuous period of at least eighteen months prior to the service of the complaint by reason of incompatibility; 3) Adultery; 4) Fraudulent contract of marriage; 5) Desertion for one year with total neglect of duty; 6) Disappearance for 7 years without being heard from; 7) Habitual intemperance; 8) Repeated cruelty; 9) Conviction of a felony or sentence to life imprisonment; 10) Institutional confinement for judicial insanity for a period of five years.

Court: Superior Court
Residence: 1 year
Statute: Connecticut States Annotated 46-32.

Connecticut's divorce law, Sec. 46-47 of the General Statute, gives the following rule for determining when a marriage has broken down: "When the parties (i.e., the husband and the wife) submit a written stipulation that their marriage has broken down irretrievably, or when both parties are physically present in court and have submitted an agreement concerning the custody, care, education, visitation, maintenance and support of their children, the testimony of either party in support of that conclusion shall be sufficient and the court shall make a finding that such marriage breakdown has occurred . . ."

DELAWARE

Grounds:

*1) The court shall enter a decree of divorce when it finds that the marriage is irretrievably broken.

A marriage is irretrievably broken where there has been a voluntary separation, or a separation caused by respondent's misconduct, or separation caused by respondent's mental illness, or separation caused by incompatibility, where reconciliation is improbable.

Court: Family Court
Statute: Delaware Code Annotated 13-1505.
Residence: 6 months

DISTRICT OF COLUMBIA

Grounds:

*1) Voluntary separation for one year without cohabitation; 2) Adultery; 3) Actual or constructive desertion for one year; 4) Conviction of felony and sentence of not less than two years for which spouse served in whole or in part; 5) Decree of divorce from bed and board which resulted in continued separation of the parties for one year may be converted into a decree of absolute divorce on the application of the innocent spouse.

Court: Superior Court
Statute: D.C. Code Annotated 16-904.
Residence: 1 year

FLORIDA

Grounds:

*1) Irretrievable breakdown of marriage; 2) Adjudication of one of the parties as mentally incompetent at least three years prior to the proceedings for dissolution of marriage.

Court: Circuit Court
Statute: Florida Statutes 61.052.
Residence: 6 months

---

* Indicates that this is a "no-fault" ground.

GEORGIA

Grounds:

*1) Irretrievable breakdown of the marriage; 2) Incestuous intermarriage; 3) Lack of comprehension or mental capacity at the time of the marriage; 4) Force, menace, duress or fraud in obtaining the marriage; 5) Impotence at the time of the marriage; 6) Pregnancy caused by another man at the time of marriage; 7) Adultery; 8) Desertion for one year; 9) Conviction for a crime involving moral turpitude for which the spouse is sentenced to imprisonment for two years immediately prior to the commencement of the divorce action; 10) Habitual drunkenness; 11) Physical or mental cruelty; 12) Adjudicated insanity or incurable mental illness and confinement to an institution for two years prior to the commencement of the action; 13) Habitual drug addiction.

Irretrievable breakdown is interpreted as where either or both parties are unable or refuse to cohabit and there are no prospects for reconciliation. (223 S.E. 2d 802.)

Court: Superior Court
Statute: Georgia Code Annotated 30-102.
Residence: 6 months

HAWAII

Grounds:

*1) The marriage is irretrievably broken; 2) The parties have lived apart for a continuous period of two years or more, and there is no reasonable likelihood that cohabitation will be resumed; 3) The parties have lived separate and apart under a decree of separation from bed and board entered by any court of competent jurisdiction, and the term of separation has expired, and no reconciliation has been effected; 4) The parties have lived separate and apart for a period of two years or more under a decree of separate maintenance entered by any court of competent jurisdiction, and no reconciliation has been effected.

Court: Circuit Court
Property distribution rule upon divorce: By community property rule
Statute: Hawaii Revised Statutes 580-41.
Residence: 6 months

IDAHO

Grounds:

1) Adultery; 2) Extreme cruelty; 3) Desertion; 4)Willful neglect for 1 year; 5) Habitual intemperance for 1 year; 6) Conviction of a felony; 7) Idiocy or insanity for which the spouse is confined in an insane asylum for three years or more prior to the commencement of the divorce action. *8) Irreconcilable differences. (Irreconcilable differences are those grounds which are determined by the court to be substantial reason for not continuing the marriage and which make it appear that the marriage should be dissolved.) *9) Living separate and apart continuously without cohabitation for five years prior to the commencement of the divorce action.

Court: District Court
Property distribution rule upon divorce: By community property rule
Statute: Idaho Code 32-603.
Residence: 6 weeks

---

* Indicates this is a "no-fault" ground.

ILLINOIS

Grounds:

*1) Irreconcilable differences have caused the irretrievable breakdown of the marriage or reconciliation has failed or further attempts at reconciliation are impractical and the spouses have been living separate and apart without cohabitation for 2 years. (If both spouses consent, the time period becomes 6 months) 2) Impotence of either party at the time of marriage and prior to commencement of the divorce action; 3) Prior existing marriage; 4) Adultery; 5) Desertion for one year; 6) Alcoholism or drug addiction for two years; 7) Attempt on the life of the other spouse by poison or other means showing malice; 8) Repeated physical or mental cruelty; 9) Conviction of a felony; 10) Infected the other with a communicable venereal disease.

Court: Circuit Court
Statute: Illinois Hurd Annotated Statutes 40-401.
Residence: 90 days

INDIANA

Grounds:

*1) Irretrievable breakdown; 2) The conviction of a felonious or infamous crime during marriage; 3) Impotence at the time of the marriage; 4) Idiocy or insanity of either party for a period of a least two years.

Court: Superior Court/Circuit Court
Statute: Indiana Statutes Annotated 31-1-11.5-1.
Residence: 6 months

IOWA

Grounds:

*1) Breakdown of the marriage relationship to the extent that the legitimate objects of matrimony have been destroyed and there remains no reasonable likelihood that the marriage can be preserved.

Court: District Court
Statute: Iowa Code Annotated 598.17.
Residence: 1 year

KANSAS

Grounds:

*1) Incompatibility; 2) Abandonment for one year; 3) Adultery; 4) Mental or physical cruelty; 5) Habitual drunkenness; 6) Willful neglect; 7) Conviction and imprisonment of felony during marriage; 8) Confinement in an institution for mental illness for a period of three years, which need not be continuous; or a judicial determination of mental illness or incapacity for more than three years with a finding by at least two of three physicians appointed by the court before whom the action is pending, that the defendant has a poor prognosis for recovery.

Court: District Court
Statute: Kansas Statutes Annotated 60-1601..
Residence: 60 days

KENTUCKY

Grounds:

*1) Irretrievable breakdown.

A finding of irretrievable breakdown is a determination that there is no reasonable prospect of reconciliation.

Court: Circuit Court
Statute: Kentucky Revised Statutes Annotated 403.110.
Residence: 180 days

---

* Indicates this is a "no-fault" ground.

LOUISIANA

Grounds:

*1) Continuous separation for one year; *2) That a spouse (or both) desires a divorce; 3) Adultery; 4) Conviction and sentence for felony to a death sentence or imprisonment at hard labor; 5) If there is no reconciliation one year from judgment of bed and board divorce, plaintiff in that action is entitled to obtain absolute divorce; if plaintiff does not act, the other spouse may obtain divorce one year and sixty days from the bed and board divorce.

Court: District Court
Property Distribution upon divorce: Based on community property rule.
Statute: Louisiana Civil Code Annotated 9-301.
Residence: 6 months

MAINE

Grounds:

*1) Irreconcilable marital differences; 2) Adultery; 3) Impotence; 4) Mental or physical cruelty; 5) Desertion for three consecutive years prior to the commencement of the action; 6) Habitual drunkenness or drug addiction; 7) Nonsupport or neglect to provide suitable maintenance for needy spouse; 8) Confinement in a mental institution for at least seven consecutive years prior to the commencement of the divorce action.

For the 'irreconcilable marital differences' ground, both parties are required to have received counseling by a professional counselor, approved by the court as qualified, and a copy of the counselor's report made available to the court.

Court: District Court
Statute: Maine Revised Statutes Annotated 19-691.
Residence: 6 months

MARYLAND

Grounds:

*1) Voluntary living apart for twelve consecutive months without reasonable expectation of reconciliation;*2) Living separate and apart without cohabitation or interruption for three years; 3) Impotence at the time of marriage; 4) Any cause rendering marriage void, e.g. a prior existing marriage or bigamy; 5) Adultery; 6) Continuous abandonment for twelve months which is without reasonable expectation of reconciliation; 7) Conviction of a felony or misdemeanor, with sentence of at least three years or an indeterminate sentence with 12 months already served; 8) Idiocy or insanity for which the other spouse is confined in an institution for not less than three years.

Court: Equity Courts
Statute: Maryland Annotated Code 16-24.
Residence: 1 year

MASSACHUSETTS:

Grounds:

1) Adultery; 2) Impotence; 3) Desertion for one year; 4) Alcoholism or drug addiction; 5) Mental or physical cruelty; 6) Willful neglect or nonsupport of wife by husband when he is able to do so; 7) Sentence to the federal penal institutions or reformatory institution for life or for five years or more; *8) An irretrievable breakdown of marriage.

Court: Superior Court/Probate Court
Statute: Massachusetts Laws Annotated Chapter 208.
Residence: 1 year

---

* Indicates this is a "no-fault" ground.

MICHIGAN

Grounds:

*1) Breakdown of the marriage relationship to the extent that the objects of matrimony have been destroyed and there remains no reasonable likelihood that the marriage can be preserved.

The Michigan statute makes it deliberately easy to prepare the divorce papers by providing that in the preparation of a complaint for divorce, all that a petitioner is required to do is to repeat the above statement used in the statute. The complaint or petition, it states, "shall make no other explanation on the grounds for divorce than by the use of the statutory language."

Court: Circuit Court
Statute: Michigan Statutes Annotated 25-86
Residence: 6 months

MINNESOTA

Grounds:

*1) Irretrievable breakdown of the marriage relationship. The court is required to make a finding of "irretrievable breakdown" upon presentation of evidence of *any* of the following:

a. A course of conduct harmful to the relationship of the party seeking dissolution; or
b. Sentence to imprisonment during the course of marriage; or
c. Habitual drunkenness or drug addiction for a period of one year prior to the commencement of divorce action; or
d. Commitment to mental institution; or
e. Uninterrupted separation, under an order or decree of separate maintenance, for one year prior to the commencement of the divorce action; or
*f. Serious discord between the marital parties.

Court: District Court
Statute: Minnesota Statutes Annotated 518-06.
Residence: 6 months

MISSISSIPPI

Grounds:

1) Impotence at the time of marriage; 2) Adultery; 3) Imprisonment; 4) Desertion for a continuous period of one year; 5) Habitual drunkenness 6) Drug addiction; 7) Repeated cruel and inhuman treatment; 8) Insanity or idiocy at the time of the marriage; 9) Prior existing marriage; 10) Pregnancy caused by another man at the time of marriage; 11) Incestuous marriage; 12) Confinement in an institution for at least three years for insanity; *13) Irreconcilable differences.

Court: Chancery Court
Statute: Mississippi Code Annotated 93-5-1.
Residence: 6 months

MISSOURI

Grounds:

*1) Irretrievable breakdown of the marriage with no likelihood that the marriage can be preserved.

Court: Circuit Court
Statute: Statutes Annotated Missouri Statutes 452.305.
Residence: 90 days

---

* Indicates this is a "no-fault" ground

MONTANA

Grounds:

*1) Irretrievable breakdown of the marriage and serious marital discord which adversely affects the attitude of both spouses toward the marriage and no reasonable prospect of reconciliation, and living separate and apart for 180 days prior to filing for divorce.

Court: District Court

Statute: Montana Revised Code Annotated 48-316.

Residence: 90 days

NEBRASKA

Grounds:

*1) Irretrievable breakdown of the marriage.

A marriage 'irretrievably breaks down' when a personal relationship between the married parties has deteriorated to the point that the parties can no longer live together.

Court: District Court

Property distribution upon divorce: based on community property rule.

Statute: Revised Statutes of Nebraska 42-361.

Residence: 1 year

NEVADA

Grounds:

1) Insanity existing for two years before the commencement of the action. *2) Living separate an apart for one year without cohabitation; *3) Incompatibility.

Court: District Court

Distribution of Property Upon divorce: based on community property rule

Statute: Nevada Revised Statutes 125.010.

Residence: 6 months

NEW HAMPSHIRE

Grounds:

1) Impotence; 2) Adultery; 3) Repeated mental or physical cruelty; 4) Conviction and actual confinement in prison for a felony; 5) Disappearance without being heard from for two consecutive years; 6) Habitual drunkenness for two years; 7) Joining religious sect disbelieving in marriage and refusal by such spouse to cohabit with the other for six months; 8) Abandonment without cause by either party and refusal to cohabit for two years; 9) Nonsupport by husband; 10) Voluntary absence of wife from her husband without his consent for two years; 11) Wife going to live outside of the state and remaining away from husband for ten years, without his consent and without returning to claim her marriage rights; 12) Husband being an alien or citizen of another state, and wife living separate in the state of New Hampshire for two years while the husband left the United States to become a citizen of some foreign country and did not return to the state or make suitable provision for the wife's support.

*13) Irreconcilable differences which have caused the irremediable breakdown of the marriage. If one spouse resolutely refuses to continue and it is clear from the passage of time or other circumstances that there is no reasonable possibility of a change of heart, there is an irremediable breakdown of the marriage. Desrochers v. Desrochers, 347 A.2d 150.

Court: Superior Court

Statute: New Hampshire Revised Statutes 458.7.

Residence: 1 year

---

* Indicates this is a "no-fault" ground

NEW JERSEY

Grounds:

*1) Separation for eighteen consecutive months, with no apparent reasonable prospect of reconciliation existing; 2) Adultery; 3) Willful and continued desertion for twelve months or more and no cohabitation; 4) Extreme physical cruelty or mental cruelty which endangers the safety or health of the plaintiff and makes cohabitation by the complaining party improper or unreasonable; 5) Drug addition or habitual drunkenness for twelve consecutive months after marriage; 6) Institutionalization for mental illness for twenty-four consecutive months after the marriage; 7) Imprisonment of the defendant for eighteen consecutive months after the marriage; if action is not commenced until after the defendant's release, proof that the parties have not resumed cohabitation is required; 8) Deviant or unnatural sexual conduct by the defendant without consent of the plaintiff.

Court: Superior Court

Statute: New Jersey Statutes Annotated 2A:34-2.

Residence: 1 year

NEW MEXICO

Grounds:

[*] *1) Incompatibility. 2) Cruel and inhuman treatment; 3) Adultery; 4) Abandonment.
Incompatibility exists when the level of marital discord or conflict of personalities is so high that it prevents any reasonable expectation of reconciliation.

Court: District Court

Property Distribution upon Divorce: based on community property rule

Statute: New Mexico Statutes Annotated 22-7-1.

Residence: 6 months

NEW YORK

Grounds:

1) Mental or physical cruelty; 2) Abandonment for a continuous period of one year; 3) Adultery; 4) Confinement of defendant in prison for three or more years after the marriage; 5) Living apart for a period of at least one year pursuant to a decree or judgment of separation. 6) Living apart for a period of at least one year pursuant to a written separation agreement.

Court: Supreme Court

Property Distribution upon Divorce: based on equitable distribution rule.

Statute: New York Domestic Relations Laws, Section 170.

Residence: 1 year

NORTH CAROLINA

Grounds:

*1) Continuous separation and living apart for one year; 2) Adultery; 3) Impotence; 4) Pregnancy caused by another man at the time of the marriage; 5) Engaging in deviant sexual intercourse or unnatural behavior, such as intercourse with a person of the same sex or a beast; 6) Living apart for 3 consecutive years without cohabitation by reason of incurable insanity of one spouse and his confinement in an institution for 3 consecutive years; certified incurable insanity, whether confined or otherwise.

Court: Superior Court

Statute: North Carolina General Statutes 50-5.

Residence: 6 months

---

* Indicates this is a "no-fault" ground

NORTH DAKOTA

Grounds:

*1) Irreconcilable differences. Irreconcilable differences are those grounds which are determined by the court to be substantial reason for not continuing the marriage; 2) Adultery; 3) Repeated cruelty; 4) Willful desertion for a period of one year; 5) Willful neglect or nonsupport by spouse for a period of one year; 6) Alcoholism for a period of one year; 7) Conviction of a felony; 8) Confinement for insanity for a period of 3 years in an institution; 9) Decree of separation in existence for more than four years and reconciliation improbable.

Court: District Court
Statute: North Dakota Code 14-05.03.
Residence: 6 months

OHIO

Grounds:

*1) Incompatibility, unless denied by the other spouse; or *2) Uninterrupted living apart for one year without cohabitation; 3) Prior existing marriage; 4) Willful absence for one year; 5) Adultery; 6) Impotence; 7) Extreme cruelty; 8) Fraudulent marriage contract; 9) Willful neglect of duty; 10) Habitual drunkenness; 11) Conviction and actual imprisonment of a spouse as of the time of the filing of the petition for divorce; 12) Procurement of a divorce outside the state. (This releases the party who procures it from the obligations of marriage, while such obligations remain binding upon the other party.)

Court: Courts of Common Pleas
Statute: Ohio Revised Code Annotated 3105.01.
Residence: 6 months

OKLAHOMA

Grounds:

*1) Incompatibility; 2) Abandonment for a period of one year; 3) Adultery; 4) Impotence; 5) Pregnancy caused by another man at time of marriage; 6) Repeated acts of cruelty; 7) Fraudulent marriage contract; 8) Habitual drunkenness; 9) Willful neglect or nonsupport by spouse; 10) Imprisonment for felony; 11) Procurement of divorce decree outside the state which does not in this State release the other party from the obligations of the marriage; 12) Idiocy or insanity for five years.

Court: District Court
Property Distribution upon Divorce: based on community property rule
Statute: Oklahoma Statutes Annotated 12-1271.
Residence: 6 month

OREGON

Grounds:

*1) Irreconcilable differences between the parties have (in the judgment of one or both parties) caused the irremediable breakdown of the marriage.

Court: Circuit Court
Property Distribution upon Divorce: based on community property rule
Residence: 6 months

PENNSYLVANIA

Grounds:

*1) Irretrievable breakdown of the marriage with the spouses living separate and apart without cohabitation for 2 years; or *2) irretrievable breakdown of the marriage and the spouses have both filed affidavits that they consent to the divorce. 3) Prior existing marriage; 4) Adultery; 5) Desertion for one year; 6) Repeated

---

* Indicates this is a "no fault ground.

acts of cruelty; 7) Indignities to the person so as to render the condition of the injured spouse intolerable and life burdensome; 8) Conviction and actual imprisonment for two years; 9) Insanity or serious mental disorder with confinement in a mental institution for at least 18 months immediately before the filing of the complaint.

Court: Courts of Common Pleas
Property Distribution upon Divorce: based on community property rule
Statute: Pennsylvania Statutes Annotated 23-10.
Residence: 6 months

RHODE ISLAND

Grounds:

*1) The parties have lived separate and apart for three years without cohabitation; *2) Irreconcilable differences which have caused the irremediable breakdown of the marriage; 3) Impotence; 4) Adultery; 5) Repeated acts of cruelty; 6) Willful desertion for five years or for a shorter period "in the discretion of the court."; 7) Habitual or prolonged drunkenness; 8) Drug addiction; 9) Nonsupport by husband for one year; 10) Prior existing marriage or incestuous contract.

Court: Family Court
Statute: Rhode Island General Laws Annotated 15-5-1.
Residence: 1 year

SOUTH CAROLINA

Grounds:

*1) Living apart without cohabitation for one year; 2) Adultery; 3) Desertion for one year; 4) Physical cruelty; 5) Habitual drunkenness or narcotic addiction.

Court: Circuit Court
Statute: South Carolina Code Annotated 20-101.
Residence: 1 year

SOUTH DAKOTA

Grounds:

*1) Irreconcilable differences which have caused the irretrievable breakdown of the marriage; 2) Adultery; 3) Repeated acts of cruelty; 4) Desertion for one year; 5) Nonsupport or willful neglect for one year; 6) Habitual intemperance; 7) Conviction of a felony.

Court: Circuit Court
Statute: South Dakota Compiled Laws Annotated 25-4-2.
Residence: must be resident of State at time of filing.

TENNESSEE

Grounds:

*1) Irreconcilable differences; or *2) living separate and apart without cohabitation for 2 years when there are no minor children; 3) Impotence at the time of the marriage; 4) Prior existing marriage; 5) Adultery; 6) Willful desertion — for one year; 7) Conviction of a felony; 8) Attempt on the life of the spouse by poison or other means; 9) Pregnancy caused by another man at the time of the marriage; 10) Habitual drunkenness or use of narcotic drugs during the course of marriage; 11) Cruel and inhuman treatment;

Court: Circuit Courts/Chancery Court
Statute: Tennessee Code Annotated 36-801, 802.
Residence: 6 months

---

* Indicates this is a "no-fault" ground.

TEXAS

Grounds:

*1) Insupportability. On the petition of either party to a marriage, a divorce may be decreed without regard to fault if the marriage has become insupportable because of discord or conflict of personalities that destroys the legitimate ends of the marriage relationship and prevents any reasonable expectation of reconciliation. 2) Living apart without cohabitation for at least three years; 3) Cruelty; 4) Adultery; 5) Conviction of a felony since marriage and imprisonment for at least one year without pardon; 6) Abandonment for at least one year; 7) Confinement of spouse in a mental hospital for mental disorder for at least three years without prospect of recovery by spouse.

Court: District Court
Property Distribution upon Divorce: based on community property rule
Statute: Texas Family Code 3.01.
Residence: 1 year

UTAH

Grounds:

*1) Irreconcilable differences in the marriage; or *2) living separated and apart without cohabitation for 3 years under a judicial decree of separation. 3) Impotence at the time of the marriage; 4) Adultery; 5) Willful desertion for more than one year; 6) Willful neglect or nonsupport by spouse who is capable of providing support; 7) Habitual drunkenness of defendant; 8) Conviction of defendant for felony; 9) Mental or physical cruelty to plaintiff by defendant; 10) Incurable insanity which is adjudicated to be so by legal authorities of this or some other state.

Court: District Court
Statute: Utah Code Annotated 30-3-1.
Residence: 3 months

VERMONT

Grounds:

1) Adultery; 2) Sentence and actual confinement in prison for three years or more at the time of the action; 3) Intolerable severity or extreme cruelty; 4) Willful desertion; 5) Nonsupport, refusal or neglect to provide suitable maintenance for the other; 6) Incurable insanity and confinement in a mental institution; *7) Living apart for six consecutive months and court finding that resumption of marital relations is not reasonably probably.

Court: Superior Court
Property Distribution upon Divorce: based on equitable distribution
Statute: Vermont Revised Statutes Annotated 15-551.
Residence: 6 months

VIRGINIA

Grounds:

1) Adultery, sodomy or buggery; 2) Conviction and actual confinement in prison for felony where cohabitation was not resumed after such confinement; 3) Willful desertion for one year; *4) Continuously living separate and apart from the spouse without any cohabitation for one year.

Court: Circuit Court
Statute: Code of Virginia 20-91.
Residence: 1 year

---

* Indicates this is a "no-fault" ground.

WASHINGTON

Grounds:

*1) The marriage is irretrievably broken.

"When a party who is a resident of this state or who is a member of the Armed Forces and is stationed in this state, petitions for a dissolution of marriage, and alleges that the marriage is irretrievably broken and when ninety days have elapsed since the petition was filed and from the date when service of summons was made upon the respondent or the first publication of summons was made, the court shall . . . enter a decree of dissolution (if the other party either joins in the petition or does not deny that the marriage is irretrievably broken) . . ."

Court: Superior Court

Property Distribution upon Divorce: based on community property rule

Statute: Washington Revised Code 26.09.030.

Residence: Spouse filing for divorce must be a resident of state at time of filing.

WEST VIRGINIA

Grounds:

1) Adultery; 2) Conviction of a felony; 3) Willful abandonment or desertion for six months; 4) Cruel and inhuman treatment whether mental or physical in nature, which make continued cohabitation unsafe or intolerable; 5) Habitual drunkenness during the course of marriage; 6) Narcotic addiction during the course of marriage; 7) One year living separate and apart without cohabitation and interruption, whether by voluntary act of one party or by mutual consent; 8) Incurable insanity for which the party is confined in an institution for three years prior to the filing of complaint; 9) Abuse or neglect of a child of the parties; *10) Irreconcilable differences.

Court: Circuit Court

Statute: West Virginia Code Annotated 48-2-4.

Residence: 1 year

WISCONSIN

Grounds:

*1) Irretrievable breakdown of the marriage.

The irretrievable breakdown of the marriage may be shown by: 1) a joint petition by both spouses requesting a divorce on this ground; or 2) living separate and apart for 12 months immediately prior to filing; or 3) if the court finds an irretrievable breakdown of the marriage with no possible chance of reconciliation.

Court: Circuit Court

Statute: Wisconsin Statutes Annotated 247.07.

Residence: 6 months

WYOMING

Grounds:

*1) Irreconcilable Differences.

2) Confinement for incurable insanity for two years.

Court: District Court

Statute: Wyoming Statutes Annotated 20-2-104.

Residence: 60 days

---

* Indicates this is a "no-fault" ground.

APPENDIX D

Some Relevant Glossary Of Legal Terms

ABANDONMENT- The act of leaving a husband or wife. Also called "desertion."

ABATEMENT- A lessening or decrease (e.g., tax abatement)

ACKNOWLEDGMENT- A declaration, in front of a person who is legally qualified to administer an oath (such as a Notary Public), that a document bearing your signature was actually signed by you.

ACTION- A lawsuit or proceeding in a court of law.

ADDENDUM- Something added afterwards.

AD VALOREM- Latin for "based upon the value." Example: property taxes.

ADVERSE POSSESSION- The occupancy or enjoyment of property, in spite of and against the will of the person who has legal title.

AFFIDAVIT- A statement in writing, sworn to before a person authorized to administer oath, such as a Notary Public.

ALLEGATIONS- The claims or charges made in a lawsuit against the other party.

ALIMONY- The allowance ordered by the court to be paid by a husband for the support and maintenance of his wife (as opposed to the children) usually after both parties have separated or divorced.

ANSWER- A formal response to the allegations made in a complaint or petition.

ANNULMENT- A legal action which has the result of treating a marriage as if it had never occurred.

ANTE-NUPTIAL CONTRACT OR AGREEMENT- Contract made before marriage, setting out the rights and obligations of each if the marriage ends in divorce. Same as pre-nuptial.

APPEAL- A resort to a higher court for the purpose of obtaining a review of a lower court decision and a reversal of the lower court judgment or the granting of a new trial.

APPEARANCE- The coming into a case by a party summoned in a court action; to come into a case upon being summoned, either by one's self or through one's attorney; to voluntarily submit one's self to the jurisdiction of the court (made either in person or by filing a formal document, such as an answer or a waiver).

ASSIGNEE- The person to whom a property or the rights to it are transferred.

ASSIGNOR- The person who assigns (transfers) a property right to another person.

BASTARDY PROCEEDINGS- Court action against the father of a child born out of wedlock to compel support for the child.

BIGAMY- The crime (under U.S. law) of having two living legal spouses at the same time.

BREACH OF CONTRACT- Failure to perform a duty or fulfill an obligation called for in a contract.

CASE LAW- The body of law created by appellate court decisions. The case law may interpret written laws, or it may create law where there are no statutes.

COHABITATION- The act of living together by two persons of opposite sex who are not married to each other.

COLLATERAL- Something that is additional or incidental to the main issue that is being discussed e.g., child custody or support payments are 'collateral issues' in dissolving marriages.

COLLUSION- A secret agreement to defraud someone, or to do certain things that are illegal or against public morality.

COMMINGLING (OF ASSETS)- A situation where a husband and wife have so mixed up the separate property of each that it is difficult to know which one separately belongs to whom.

COMMON LAW MARRIAGE- A marriage in which there has been no formal ceremony or marriage license.

COMMUNITY PROPERTY- As defined by most states which have adopted the "community property" system, community property is any property or asset acquired by the husband and/or the wife from the time of their marriage onward (usually excluding the property acquired either before the marriage or by gift or inheritance). As of this writing, community property states are the following: Arizona, California, Idaho, Louisiana, Nevada, New Mexico, Texas, Washington and Wisconsin.

COMMUNITY PROPERTY RULE- The rule that the sum total of whatever is considered the community of a married couple, would be divided ***equally*** between both spouses, under the theory that both spouses make equal contribution to a marriage, the husband as a breadwinner, and the wife as the homemaker so that the husband is freed to engage in his job.

COMPETENT PERSON- A person who is mentally fit, and therefore considered legally capable of entering into a contract.

COMPLAINT-The main document in a civil case court action made out by the plaintiff ("complainant") listing the complaints and allegations and other relevant facts related to the plaintiff's case. The person who first makes out the complaint against another, is called the complainant or plaintiff, and the party against whom he makes out the complaint is the defendant or respondent. (Same as PETITIONER)

CONCLUSIONS OF LAW- A judge's opinion of what the law says which applied in a given situation.

CONFORMING THE COPIES- Filling in information from the original pleading or document on the reproduced copies of the document. When conforming a copy as to a signature, it's customary to put an /s/ in front of the name to indicate it was not an original signature on the copy.

CONSIDERATION- The thing of value that is given or offered to induce a person to enter into a contract or agreement.

CONTESTED- Differences that must be settled before a court.

CONTESTED DIVORCE- A divorce where at least one issue has not been settled prior to court.

CONTINUANCE- A postponement granted by the judge of a scheduled matter to a later date on the court's calendar.

CONTRIBUTORY RETIREMENT PLAN- Where both the employee and the employer contribute funds to a retirement plan for the benefit of the employee.

CORE CONSIDERATIONS- Those basics considered by the courts in making a property division and/or awarding alimony in a divorce case: age, health, sex, education, earning capacity, future prospects, children to care for, and any other similar relevant considerations, such as fault in causing the breakdown of the marriage in some states.

COUNTER CLAIM- A complaint (or petition) filed by a defendant (or respondent) which states claims against the plaintiff (or petitioner).

CUSTODIAL PARENT- The parent who has custody of the child; the one with whom a child normally lives.

DECREE- The title of the final ruling in a case, as in FINAL DECREE OF DIVORCE.

DEFAULT ORDER/JUDGMENT- An order or judgment of a court based only on the plaintiff's (or petitioner's) case. One party (the petitioner) shall have filed suit and served the defendant (or respondent) with notice of the suit, and the defendant (or respondent) shall not have answered the allegations or made an appearance in the case.

DEFENDANT- The person who defends against a lawsuit brought against him or her by another. (Same as RESPONDENT.)

DEPOSITIONS- Questions asked by both plaintiff and defendant (or their attorneys) and answered by a prospective witness, before a court reporter, and under oath. A form of "discovery."

DISCOVERY- The right of either party to learn from all who have information, anything which is relevant to the suit. Any of the formal procedures for obtaining information important to a case, such as notice to produce documents, written interrogatories, and depositions.

DISCRETION- Using one's own good judgment, within reasonable bounds.

DISSOLUTION OF MARRIAGE- A legal judgment that terminates a marriage. (Same as divorce).

DIVORCE- Legal dissolution (termination) of a marriage.

DOCKET- The court's book containing a brief entry of the important events in each case with their dates. Also, a list or calendar of cases set for hearings.

DOMICILE- One's permanent or legal home, as opposed to one's temporary place of abode.

EARNED INCOME- Money which is received in return for labor. Interest, alimony, child support, retirement pay, Social Security payments, welfare payments and trust income are not "earned income."

ENTIRETY- The phrase "ownership (or tenancy) by the entirety" is used to describe a situation when two ore more persons (but more commonly a husband a wife) jointly own a real property, so that the property cannot be divided between themselves. Hence, if one of the parties should die, the whole property goes to the survivor(s).

EQUITABLE CLAIMS- This refers to a right or claim which is enforceable although not based upon a written contract.

EQUITABLE DIVISION- A method of property division in a divorce (or dissolution of marriage) which is generally based on a variety of factors in an attempt to allocate a fair and just amount of property to each spouse.

EQUITY- Fairness and justice.

ESTATE- The sum total of the property, both real and personal, owned by a decedent (the dead person) at the time of his death.

ESTATE BY THE- When two people own property in this manner, each of them owns the whole property. Ordinarily husbands and wives own property by the entirety with the right of survivorship so that when one dies, the other simply becomes the sole owner of the whole property.

EX-CONTRACTU- Latin term meaning "from contract." Used to describe a court action or obligation that arises out of a contract or contractual obligation.

EXECUTION- The completion of a document (such as a will, contract, or agreement) by officially signing it.

FAULT- As used in divorce proceedings, "fault" refers to the actions of the parties with respect to the cause or reason for divorce, such as adultery, alcoholism, and so on.

FAULT-BASED DIVORCE- A divorce which may only be granted on a showing that one of the spouses was guilty of some form of marital misconduct.

FINDINGS OF FACT- This is a statement by a judge as to his or her belief of the facts presented during the trial.

FOREIGN DECREE- Ordinarily, refers to a decree of another state. For example, a New York decree would be a foreign decree to the California court.

FIRST IMPRESSION- An original question in a particular state which has not been decided by an appellate court in that state.

GROSS INCOME- The total income a person receives before deductions for taxes, retirement, insurance, and so on.

GROUNDS- The legal basis or reasons for the divorce (or *dissolution of marriage*). The grounds may be no-fault or fault-based.

HEARING- Any proceeding before a court where testimony is given or arguments heard.

HOLD-HARMLESS- A phrase used to describe an agreement by which one person agrees to assume full liability for an ogligation and protect another from any loss or expense based on that obligation.

INCORPORATED INTO- As used mostly in settlement agreements or divorce judgements, the term refers to the parties' agreement to a divorce which is specifically referred to in the court decree and which actually becomes a part of the decree.

INDEMNITY- An "indemnity" provision between two parties provides that if the one who agreed to assume a liability does not pay, the other must pay, instead. If this happens, the one who should have paid must reimburse the paying party. It is frequently used to cover debt obligations, tax liability or mortgage payments in a divorce agreement.

INTEGRATED BARGAIN- A term used by the courts in interpreting divorce agreements from which a later dispute has arisen. It is well settled that generally a court cannot change a property division, but generally a court can change support payments. Most divorce agreements cover both provisions. If the court feels that both types of provisions were part of a total bargain, it will not change the support provision.

INTERROGATORIES- Questions one party asks another, in writing, which must be answered, in writing, under oath. A form of "discovery," but may only be used by one named party to the suit to another named party to the suit.

IMPLIED CONTRACT- Implied contracts are of two basic types: implied "in fact" and implied "in law." A contract implied "in fact," is one whose terms are inferred (implied) from the acts, conducts, and apparent intentions of the parties in a given situation. (Example: Mr. A steps into a taxicab and hands the driver a certain address. If the driver transports Mr. A to that address, Mr. A is reasonably expected, by implication "in fact," to pay a fare, although he had not expressly promised to do so). A contract is implied "in law" when, under certain circumstances, Mr. A has conferred a benefit upon Mr. B, which therefore implicitly entitles Mr. A to receive a reasonable value from Mr. B in return, if Mr. B's retention of the benefit would constitute an unjust enrichment at Mr. A's expense. (Example: Dr. A, a physician, renders first aid to Mr. B while Mr. B is unconscious as a result of an accident. Mr. B is expected, by contract implied "in law", to pay Dr. A the fair value of the service he received from him.)

IRRETRIEVABLE BREAKDOWN- Differences that cannot be reconciled; the ground for requesting a dissolution of marriage under no-fault system.

JOINT LEGAL CUSTODY- A form of custody of minor children in which the parties share the responsibilities and major decisions relating to the child. Generally, one parent is awarded actual physical custody of the child and the other parent is awarded liberal visitation rights.

JOINT PHYSICAL CUSTODY- A form of custody of minor children in which the parents share the actual physical custody of the child, generally alternating the custody.

JOINT PROPERTY- Property which is held or titled in the name of more than one person. (See *joint tenancy, community property* and *marital property.*)

JOINT TENANCY- The phrase "joint tenancy" or "joint ownership" is used to describe a situation when two or more persons (usually non-marital parties) own or hold a property in joint names, so that if any of them should die, the entire property goes to the remaining survivors.

JURISDICTION- The power or authority of a court to decide in a particular case.

LITIGATION- A court action or contest.

LEGAL SEPARATION A lawsuit to live apart and for support while the spouses are living separate and apart. May often deal with the same issues as in a divorce, but does not dissolve the marriage.

LUMP-SUM ALIMONY- Spousal support that is made in a single payment or in a fixed amount, but paid in specific installments.

MAINTENANCE- Support for a spouse provided by the other spouse. Same as alimony or spousal support.

MAJORITY- Refers to the age at which the child becomes an adult. This is governed by state statutes and generally varies from age 18 to 21. Child support generally ends when a child reaches majority.

MARITAL PROPERTY- Generally the property acquired during the marriage by the efforts of both spouses which is subject to division by a court upon divorce or dissolution.

MARITAL SETTLEMENT AGREEMENT- A written agreement entered into by divorcing spouses that spells out their rights and agreements re ,arding property, support, and children, etc. (Same as *separation agreement.*).

MATURED RETIREMENT FUND- If an employee has met all of the conditions for retirement so that he could retire and receivce his retirement payments, then his retirement has "matured", i.e., is payable.

MERGE WITH- See "incorporate into."

MOTION- A written or oral request to a court for some type of action, such as a motion to continue a trial to a later date.

NO-FAULT DIVORCE- Now adopted in almost every state in the nation, this is a concept of marital dissolution which is governed by one fundamental philosophy: replacement of the traditional concept that fault must be found with one (or both) spouses as the only basis for a divorce, with a new concept which only seeks to establish merely that the marital relationship has failed or broken down. To be awarded a divorce under most no-fault laws, you are only required to show (or just to make the claim) that you and your spouse have developed some "irreconcilable differences which have caused the irremediable breakdown of the marriage"— in other words, that there is plain inability of the parties to get along or live amicably with each other.

NON-CONTRIBUTORY- A retirement plan wherein only the employer contributes money to the account of the employee for his eventual retirement.

NON-MARITAL PROPERTY- Term used to describe separate property in some states that provide for the equitable distribution of property; generally consists of property acquired prior to a marriage and by individual gift or inheritance, either before or during a marriage. (See *marital property, community property,* and *separate property.*)

NOTARY PUBLIC- A person authorized, under the laws of the state, to administer oaths and accept acknowledgement of signatures to documents. (Such persons may usually be found in banks, in and around courthouses, real estate and lawyer's offices, often in drugstores, etc.)

NULL AND VOID- An act or pronouncement that has no legal binding or effect. (Void ab initio means the act or statement had no legal binding or effect ***from the beginning.)***

ORDER- A court's ruling on some matter before it, generally, in writing and signed by the judge.

PALIMONY- The payment of support by one lover to another when the persons were never married.

PARTITION- Divide.

PARTY- A person directly involved in a lawsuit; either a plaintiff/petitioner or a defendant/respondent.

PERSONAL JURISDICTION- The power or authority of a court to make orders regarding a certain person and to have those orders legally enforced.

PETITION- A written statement, often sworn to by the maker before a Notary Public, in which the maker (the "petitioner" or "plaintiff") lists all the facts on which he bases his court action, and the remedies he demands of the court. Basically the same as a "complaint."

PETITIONER- The person who initiates a lawsuit by filing a petition with the court. (Same as plaintiff).

PENDENTE LITE- Latin expression which means "while the action or litigation is pending." Therefore, orders made by the court (e.g., about custody, support, or alimony) pendente lite, are in fact temporary orders which will continue from the time beginning when a suit is filed and ending when there is a final decree.

PERMANENT ALIMONY- Same as "alimony."

PLAINTIFF- Same as "complainant" or "petitioner."

PLEADINGS- The plaintiff's complaint *and* the "answer" (reply) of the defendant constitute, together, the pleadings — that is, the complete allegations of both sides in a case.

POSTHUMOUS CHILD- A child born after the father's death.

POSTNUPTIAL- Something entered into by the parties ***after*** their marriage. Separation agreement is a form of postnuptial agreement.

PRAYER- That portion of a complaint or petition which contains the action or relief that the plaintiff or petitioner is requesting of the court.

PRESUMPTION- Where the court assumes something is true until one of the parties proves otherwise.

PRIMARY CARETAKER- The parent who provides the majority of the day-to-day care for a minor child.

PRO SE- Latin term meaning "for himself" or "on his own behalf." Term used generally to describe a non-lawyer who is acting for himself or representing himself in a court case.

PUBLIC POLICY- The general principles of good and evil which prevail in the society, e.g., the requirement that contracts may not undermine the institution of marriage.

QUANTUM MERUIT- Latin term meaning "according to what he / she deserves." This is a legal doctrine whereby the parties involved in an issue or dispute over the amount to be paid for a service, are considered to be entitled to receive the "reasionable" value assessed for the service rendered. Thus, for example, the court may use this doctrine to determine that a partner in a marital or non-marital relationship is entitled to receive the "reasonable" value of the household services rendered, minus the reasonable value of the compensation and support she already receives.

REHABILITATIVE ALIMONY- Alimony which is granted for a short or limited period of time, usually just long enough for the ex-spouse to get on his / her feet and get a job. It states a specific time to end, and can be extended only for good cause shown to the court.

RELIEF- Whatever you are asking the court to do for you, e.g., to grant you a divorce, award you custody or support, etc.

RESPONDENT- Same as defendant.

RESPONSE- The formal document filed by a respondent in answer to the allegations in a petition. (Same as an *answer.*)

RIGHT OF SURVIVORSHIP- The right of joint owners of a piece of property to automatically be given the other's share of the property upon the death of the other owner. For this right to apply, it must, generally, be specifically stated on any documents of title. (Example: 'joint tenancy with the right of survivorship.')

RESULTING TRUST- A trust relationship that is not expressed in any document or specifically set up, but which arises from the acts, conducts, and apparent intentions of the parties. (Example: When the title to a piece of real estate is taken in the name of Mr. A but the purchase price is paid by Mr. B who is in no way obligated to A, then a trust "results" in which A holds the property as a trustee for the benefit of B, the provider of the purchase funds.)

SEPARATE MAINTENANCE- A lawsuit for support in a situation where the spouses live separate and apart but are not presently pursuing a divorce or dissolution. (Same as *legal separation.*)

SEPARATE PROPERTY- Property belonging to only one spouse in which the other generally has no claim.

SEPARATION (LEGAL SEPARATION)- The act of living apart by a husband and wife either by a written agreement or by a court order.

SERVICE OF PROCESS- The actual act of presenting the defendant or respondent in a lawsuit with a summons (or other legal papers) to notify him or her of the lawsuit.

SETTLEMENT AGREEMENT- The written version of a settlement which resolves certain issues.

SIGNATURE- A signed name or mark on a document to identify the person who made the document.

SODOMY- Perverted sexual intercourse e.g., an intercourse with an animal.

SOLE CUSTODY- A form of child custody in which one parent is given both physical custody of the child and the right to make all of the major decisions regarding the child's upbringing, with the other parent generally awarded reasonable visitation rights. (See *joint custody* and *split custody.*)

SPLIT CUSTODY- A form of child custody in which the actual time of physical custody is split between the parents, with both retaining the rights to participate in decisions regarding the child. (See *joint custody* and *sole custody.*)

SPOUSAL SUPPORT- Financial support for a spouse provided by the other spouse. (Same as alimony or maintenance.)

STIPULATION- An item or provision in a contract; a preliminary agreement separately worked out between husband and wife with a view to incorporating the terms of that agreement into a later divorce decree.

STATUTORY LAW- Those laws written by the state legislatures which are collected in the state law Code.

SUBJECT-MATTER JURISDICTION- The power or authority of a court to decide issues relating to certain subjects. For example: a Family Court may decide issues relating to the affairs of families; divorces, annulments, separations, custody, etc.

SUBPOENA- A document which is served upon (delivered to) a person who is not directly involved in a lawsuit, requesting that he or she appear in court to give testimony.

SUMMONS- A document which is served upon (delivered to) a person who is named as a defendant or respondent in a lawsuit. The summons notifies the person that the lawsuit has been filed against him or her and tells them that they have a certain time limit in which to file an answer or response in reply.

TEMPORARY SUPPORT- This is support granted by the court (or by agreement) to the wife/husband and/or children until a final decree is granted.

TENANCY BY THE ENTIRETY- See "Entirety" above.

TENANCY IN COMMON- The holding or ownership of property by two or more persons in such terms that each of them has an ***undivided*** interest in the property, and on the death of a tenant, his undivided interest automatically passes to his heirs or devisees, and ***not*** to the other survivors in the partnership.

TENDER YEARS- A presumption that all else being equal, a child of "tender years" should go to the mother under the theory that the mother is the better custodian, especially of a small child. Most states have now discarded "tender years" and there is generally no presumption between the parents.

UNCONTESTED- Differences are settled by agreement which is presented to the court. A court decree is granted without a trial of the issues.

VENUE- Venue has to do with the county (parish, or whatever) within a state where a court action should take place as all courts of "general jurisdiction" within a state have "power" over all the residents of the state.

VERIFICATION- Written confirmation that a written statement or document is true, usually accomplished by swearing to the written confirmation.

VESTED PENSION RIGHTS- A person's pension rights are "vested" if that person has already acquired the right to retire at some future time upon certain conditions set forth in the individual plan. This gives the worker the option to let his or her contributions remain in the retirement plan and receive the benefits of retirement payments at the designated time rather than withdrawing his or her contributions and forfeiting all future rights under the retirement plan.

VISITATION- The right of a parent who does not have custody of a minor child to visit the child or have a child visit with him or her.

VOID- An act, deed, or pronouncement, which has no legal force, effect or legitimacy from the very beginning. Same as "void ab initio." When something is voidable, it means it has a legal effect or legitimacy *until* and unless someone takes an action that makes it void, or a court declares it so.

WAIVE- To relinquish or give up a right.

WAIVER- The intentional giving up of a right, usually made in writing (or implied from one's conduct).

APPENDIX E

SOME RELEVANT BIBLIOGRAPHY

1. "A Judicial Recognition of Illicit Cohabitation," 25 Hastings Law Journal, 1226 (1974)

2. "Validity of Prenuptial Contracts which Fix Alimony," 14 Georgia State Bar Journal 18 (1977)

3. "Rights in Respect of Engagement and Courtship Presents When Marriage Does Not Ensue," 46 American Law Reports, 3rd 578.

4. "Legal Import of Informal Marital Separation: A Survey of California Law and a Call for Change," 65 California Law Review 1015 (1977)

5. Marvin v. Marvin, 18 Cal. 3rd 660, 134 Cal. Rptr. 815, 818, 557, p. 2d 106.

6. Adams v. Jensen-Thomas, 18 Wash. App. 757, 571, p. 2d 958

7. Drafting the Marital Settlement Agreement: Strategies and Techniques (Practicing Law Institute, New York: 1977)

8. Tax Aspects of Divorce and Separation, 26 Tulane Tax Institute 27 (1977)

9. "Pro Se Marriage Dissolution in Connecticut — Some Considerations," 51 Connecticut Bar Journal 15 (1977)

10. "No Fault Divorce: 10 Years Later, Some Virtues, Some Flaws," The N.Y. Times, March 30, 1979 p. A22

11. "Sociologists Plumb the Secrets of Compatibility," The N.Y. Times, Nov. 14, 1978 p. C7.

12. "*A Legal Guide for Gay/Lesbian Couples*," (Addison-Wesley Publishing Co/NoLo Press)

13. "Learning to Mix Love and Money," The N.Y. Times, Feb. 16, 1981 p. B4

14. "Lawyers Troubled by Rehabilitation Concept in Marvin Decision," The N.Y. Times, April 20, 1979 p. A18

15. "To Have and To Hold — Short of Marriage," The N.Y. Times, July 8 1980 p. B8

16. Gail J. Koff, *Love and The Law*: *A legal Guide To Relationship In The '90's*. Simon & Schuster, N.Y. (1989)

17. Tom Biracree, *How To Protect Your Spousal Rights* (Contemporary Book, Chicago: 1991)

18. N.O.W. Legal Defense and Education and Renee Cherow-O'Leary, *The State-By-State Guide To Women's Legal Rights* (McGraw-Hill, New York: 1987)

19. Lloyd T. Kelso, *North Carolina Divorce, Alimony & Child Custody With Forms* 2nd ed. (The Harrison Co. Norcross, Ga: 1989)

20. Johnette Duff and George G. Truitt, *The Spousal Equivalent Handbook*, (Sunny Beach Publications, Houston, Tx: 1991)

21. *Arkansas Domestic Relations Handbook*, Vol. I (Arkansas Bar Association), esp. Chapters 9 and 14 on Property settlement and pre-marital agreements.

22. *Amer. Jurisprudence Legal Forms* 2d, Chaps. 17, 89 & 90, "Alimony And Separation Agreements;" and "Divorce and Separation," respectively.

23. "Denver Extends Health Coverage To Partners Of Gay City Employees," N.Y. Times, Sept. 18, 1996, p. A17

24. "Gay Partners of I.B.M. Workers to Get Benefits," N.Y. Times, Sept. 20, 1996, p. A18

APPENDIX F

ORDERING YOUR SEPARATION/PROPERTY SETTLEMENT AGREEMENT FORMS

The following is a list of forms for drafting your Separation and/or Property Settlement Agreements obtainable from Do-It-Yourself Legal Publishers, the nation's original and leading self-help law publisher.
(Customers: For your convenience, just make a zerox copy of this page and send it along with your order. All prices quoted here are subject to change without notice.)

TO: **Do-It-Yourself Legal Publishers** **(legal Forms Division)**
60 Park Place Suite 1013
Newark, NJ 07102

Please send me the publisher's standard "forms package for drafting a marital written agreement as follows: [Prices: $19.90 per set]

FORM	QUANTITY (sets)	PRICE
For Separation/Property Settlement Agreement Without Minor Children	____	$________
For Separation/Property Settlement Agreement With Minor Children	____	$________
(Prices: $19.90 per set) Subtotal		________
Postage @ $4.00 per set		________
Sales Tax*		________
GRAND TOTAL		$________

Answer the following:
There's a substantial amount of marital property involved. Yes ____ No ____
Later on, I plan to file for divorce in the city and county of ______________, state of ______________
I'll file for divorce under the "fault," or the "no-fault" ground for my state *(specify)*________________________________.
There are minor children in the marriage. Yes ___ No ___
I bought your book, or read, learned about it, from this source (bookstore, library, medium): ______________________

____
(Name & address, please)
____

Enclosed is the sum of $ _____ to cover the order, which includes $4.00 per set for shipping, and local sales tax,* as applicable. ***Send this order to me:***
Mr./Mrs./Ms./Dr. ____
Address: ____
City & State: ______________________________Zip __________ Tel.# (   ) __________________

*New Jersey residents enclose 6 % sales tax.

IMPORTANT: Please do NOT rip out the page. Consider others! Just make a photocopy and send it.

APPENDIX G

PUBLICATIONS FROM DO-IT-YOURSELF LEGAL PUBLISHERS/SELFHELPER LAW PRESS

The following is a list of publications from the Do-it-Yourself Legal Publishers/Selfhelper Law Press of America. (Customers: For your convenience, just make a photocopy of this page and send it along with your order. All prices quoted here are subject to change without notice.)

1. How To Draw Up Your Own Friendly Separation/Property Settlement Agreement With Your Spouse
2. Tenant Smart: How To Win Your Tenants' Legal Rights Without A Lawyer (New York Edition)
3. How To Probate & Settle An Estate Yourself Without The Lawyers' Fees ($35)
4. How To Adopt A Child Without A Lawyer
5. How To Form Your Own Profit/Non-Profit Corporation Without A Lawyer
6. How To Plan Your 'Total' Estate With A Will & Living Will, Without a Lawyer
7. How To Declare Your Personal Bankruptcy Without A Lawyer ($29)
8. How To Buy Or Sell Your Own Home Without A Lawyer or Broker ($29)
9. How To File For Chapter 11 Business Bankruptcy Without A Lawyer ($29)
10. How To Legally Beat The Traffic Ticket Without A Lawyer (forthcoming)
11. How To Settle Your Own Auto Accident Claims Without A Lawyer ($29)
12. How To Obtain Your U.S. Immigration Visa Without A Lawyer ($25)
13. How To Do Your Own Divorce Without A Lawyer [10 Regional State-Specific Volumes] ($35)
14. How To Legally Change Your Name Without A Lawyer
15. How To Properly Plan Your 'Total' Estate With A Living Trust, Without The Lawyers' Fees ($35)
16. Legally Protect Yourself In A Gay/Lesbian Or Non-Marital Relationship With A Cohabitation Agreement
17. Before You Say 'I do' In Marriage Or Co-Habitation, Here's How To First Protect Yourself Legally
18. The National Home Mortgage Escrow Audit Kit (forthcoming) ($15.95)

Prices: Each book, except for those specifically priced otherwise, costs $25, plus $3.00 per book for postage and handling. New Jersey residents please add 6% sales tax. **ALL PRICES ARE SUBJECT TO CHANGE WITHOUT NOTICE**

CUSTOMERS: Please make and send a zerox copy of this page with your orders)

ORDER FORM

TO: **Do-it-Yourself Legal Publishers**
60 PARK PLACE ., Ste. 1013, Newark, NJ 07102

Please send me the following:

1.__________copies of ______________________________

2.__________copies of ______________________________

3.__________copies of ______________________________

4.__________copies of ______________________________

Enclosed is the sum of $____________ to cover the order. *Mail my order to:*

Mr./Mrs.//Ms/Dr. ______________________________

Address (include Zip Code please): ______________________________

Phone No. and area code: ( ) ____________________ Job: ( ) ____________________

*New Jersey residents enclose 6% sales tax.

IMPORTANT: Please do NOT rip out the page. Consider others! Just make a photocopy and send it.

INDEX